FOREWORD

The late Senator Everett Dirksen of Illinois once told me
that one could not help but draw great inspiration from
the reading of the Psalms and the Proverbs. For many
years I have made it a practice to read five Psalms and a
chapter of the book of Proverbs each day, aside from my
other Bible reading and study, and it has been a great
blessing to me.

By reading five Psalms and one chapter of Proverbs
daily, you will be able to read them through each month.
The Psalms will tell you how to get along with God, and
the Proverbs will tell you how to get along with your
fellowman. In Deuteronomy 6:5 we read, "Thou shalt love
the Lord thy God with all thine heart, and with all thy
soul, and with all thy might" (KJV). In Leviticus 19:18 we
read, "Don't seek vengeance. Don't bear a grudge; but
love your neighbor as yourself, for I am Jehovah" (TLB).
Both of these great affirmations are underlined in the
Psalms and Proverbs.

In this book you have a wonderful treat in store. May
God bless you as you begin to live in its pages.

Billy Graham

PREFACE

In a way unmatched by any other literature, the book of Psalms draws us apart from the workaday life of man, brings us into the sanctuary, and directs us into precious communion with God. The Hebrew word for Psalms is *tehillim,* which in a general way means poems of praise composed to be sung.

The book of Psalms really gives us a summary of both the Old and New Testaments. All the way through the book, and particularly in the Messianic Psalms, we find the message of the Christ to come. Our risen Lord referred to the Psalms in his last message before ascending to his Father. "When I was with you before, I told you that everything written about me . . . in the Psalms must all come true" (Luke 24:44). In Colossians 3:16, the apostle Paul tells the believers to "Let the words of Christ, in all their richness, live in your hearts and make you wise. Use his words to teach and counsel each other. Sing psalms and hymns and spiritual songs to God with thankful hearts."

While the Psalms are all divinely inspired, they were composed at different times for different occasions and have been put together rather independently of each other. King David was probably the author of most of the Psalms. In 2 Samuel 23:1 he is referred to as the "psalmist of Israel." One psalm (Psalm 90) was a prayer of Moses. Other psalms were written by Asaph, for in 2 Chronicles 29:30 Hezekiah ordered the Levites to "praise the LORD with the psalms of David and Asaph." The chronicler also calls Asaph a seer, or prophet.

David's genius is found in his poetry. His lyrics became the psalter for the early church of God. No other book, perhaps, is as helpful to a Christian's devotional life as is the book of Psalms.

The Psalms are divided into five sections, also called books. Each section concludes with "Amen" or "Hallelujah." The first section ends with Psalm 41; the second with Psalm 72; the third with Psalm 89; the fourth with Psalm 106. We have purposely not made these divisions in this devotional edition but rather have paragraphed the Psalms for the convenience of the reader using them for inspiration in his or her daily devotions.

George M. Wilson

DAY ONE

PSALM 1

¹Oh, the joys of those
   who do not follow the advice of the wicked,
   or stand around with sinners,
   or join in with scoffers.
²But they delight in doing everything the LORD wants;
   day and night they think about his law.
³They are like trees planted along the riverbank,
   bearing fruit each season without fail.
Their leaves never wither,
   and in all they do, they prosper.

⁴But this is not true of the wicked.
   They are like worthless chaff, scattered by the wind.
⁵They will be condemned at the time of judgment.
   Sinners will have no place among the godly.

⁶For the LORD watches over the path of the godly,
   but the path of the wicked leads to destruction.

PSALM 2

¹Why do the nations rage?
>Why do the people waste their time with futile
>>plans?
²The kings of the earth prepare for battle;
>the rulers plot together
against the LORD
>and against his anointed one.
³"Let us break their chains," they cry,
>"and free ourselves from this slavery."

⁴But the one who rules in heaven laughs.
>The Lord scoffs at them.
⁵Then in anger he rebukes them,
>terrifying them with his fierce fury.
⁶For the LORD declares, "I have placed my chosen king
>>on the throne
>in Jerusalem, my holy city."

⁷The king proclaims the LORD's decree:
"The LORD said to me, 'You are my son.
>Today I have become your Father.
⁸Only ask, and I will give you the nations as your
>>inheritance,
>the ends of the earth as your possession.

⁹You will break them with an iron rod
    and smash them like clay pots.' "

¹⁰Now then, you kings, act wisely!
    Be warned, you rulers of the earth!
¹¹Serve the LORD with reverent fear,
    and rejoice with trembling.
¹²Submit to God's royal son, or he will become angry,
    and you will be destroyed in the midst of your pursuits—
    for his anger can flare up in an instant.

But what joy for all who find protection in him!

PSALM 3

*A psalm of David, regarding the time David fled from his
son Absalom.*

¹O LORD, I have so many enemies;
    so many are against me.
²So many are saying,
    "God will never rescue him!"   *Interlude*

³But you, O LORD, are a shield around me,
    my glory, and the one who lifts my head high.
⁴I cried out to the LORD,
    and he answered me from his holy mountain. *Interlude*

[5]I lay down and slept.

 I woke up in safety,

  for the LORD was watching over me.

[6]I am not afraid of ten thousand enemies

 who surround me on every side.

[7]Arise, O LORD!

 Rescue me, my God!

Slap all my enemies in the face!

 Shatter the teeth of the wicked!

[8]Victory comes from you, O LORD.

 May your blessings rest on your people.   *Interlude*

PSALM 4

For the choir director: A psalm of David, to be accompanied by stringed instruments.

[1]Answer me when I call,

 O God who declares me innocent.

Take away my distress.

 Have mercy on me and hear my prayer.

[2]How long will you people ruin my reputation?

 How long will you make these groundless accusations?

 How long will you pursue lies?   *Interlude*

³You can be sure of this:
  The LORD has set apart the godly for himself.
  The LORD will answer when I call to him.

⁴Don't sin by letting anger gain control over you.
  Think about it overnight and remain silent.   *Interlude*
⁵Offer proper sacrifices,
  and trust in the LORD.

⁶Many people say, "Who will show us better times?"
  Let the smile of your face shine on us, LORD.
⁷You have given me greater joy
  than those who have abundant harvests of grain and
      wine.

⁸I will lie down in peace and sleep,
  for you alone, O LORD, will keep me safe.

PSALM 5

*For the choir director: A psalm of David, to be accompanied by
the flute.*

¹O LORD, hear me as I pray;
  pay attention to my groaning.
²Listen to my cry for help, my King and my God,
  for I will never pray to anyone but you.
³Listen to my voice in the morning, LORD.

Each morning I bring my requests to you and wait
    expectantly.

⁴O God, you take no pleasure in wickedness;
    you cannot tolerate the slightest sin.
⁵Therefore, the proud will not be allowed to stand in
      your presence,
    for you hate all who do evil.
⁶You will destroy those who tell lies.
    The LORD detests murderers and deceivers.

⁷Because of your unfailing love, I can enter your house;
    with deepest awe I will worship at your Temple.
⁸Lead me in the right path, O LORD,
    or my enemies will conquer me.
Tell me clearly what to do,
    and show me which way to turn.

⁹My enemies cannot speak one truthful word.
    Their deepest desire is to destroy others.
Their talk is foul, like the stench from an open grave.
    Their speech is filled with flattery.
¹⁰O God, declare them guilty.
    Let them be caught in their own traps.
Drive them away because of their many sins,
    for they rebel against you.

¹¹But let all who take refuge in you rejoice;

let them sing joyful praises forever.

Protect them,

so all who love your name may be filled with joy.

¹²For you bless the godly, O LORD,

surrounding them with your shield of love.

PROVERBS 1

These are the proverbs of Solomon, David's son, king of
Israel.

²The purpose of these proverbs is to teach people
wisdom and discipline, and to help them understand wise
sayings. ³Through these proverbs, people will receive
instruction in discipline, good conduct, and doing what is
right, just, and fair. ⁴These proverbs will make the simple-
minded clever. They will give knowledge and purpose to
young people.

⁵Let those who are wise listen to these proverbs and
become even wiser. And let those who understand receive
guidance ⁶by exploring the depth of meaning in these
proverbs, parables, wise sayings, and riddles.

⁷Fear of the LORD is the beginning of knowledge.
Only fools despise wisdom and discipline.

⁸Listen, my child, to what your father teaches you.

Don't neglect your mother's teaching. ⁹What you learn from them will crown you with grace and clothe you with honor.

¹⁰My child, if sinners entice you, turn your back on them! ¹¹They may say, "Come and join us. Let's hide and kill someone! Let's ambush the innocent! ¹²Let's swallow them alive as the grave swallows its victims. Though they are in the prime of life, they will go down into the pit of death. ¹³And the loot we'll get! We'll fill our houses with all kinds of things! ¹⁴Come on, throw in your lot with us; we'll split our loot with you."

¹⁵Don't go along with them, my child! Stay far away from their paths. ¹⁶They rush to commit crimes. They hurry to commit murder. ¹⁷When a bird sees a trap being set, it stays away. ¹⁸But not these people! They set an ambush for themselves; they booby-trap their own lives! ¹⁹Such is the fate of all who are greedy for gain. It ends up robbing them of life.

²⁰Wisdom shouts in the streets. She cries out in the public square. ²¹She calls out to the crowds along the main street, and to those in front of city hall. ²²"You simpletons!" she cries. "How long will you go on being simple-minded? How long will you mockers relish your mocking? How long will you fools fight the facts? ²³Come here and

listen to me! I'll pour out the spirit of wisdom upon you and make you wise.

²⁴"I called you so often, but you didn't come. I reached out to you, but you paid no attention. ²⁵You ignored my advice and rejected the correction I offered. ²⁶So I will laugh when you are in trouble! I will mock you when disaster overtakes you—²⁷when calamity overcomes you like a storm, when you are engulfed by trouble, and when anguish and distress overwhelm you.

²⁸"I will not answer when they cry for help. Even though they anxiously search for me, they will not find me. ²⁹For they hated knowledge and chose not to fear the LORD. ³⁰They rejected my advice and paid no attention when I corrected them. ³¹That is why they must eat the bitter fruit of living their own way. They must experience the full terror of the path they have chosen. ³²For they are simpletons who turn away from me—to death. They are fools, and their own complacency will destroy them. ³³But all who listen to me will live in peace and safety, unafraid of harm."

PSALM 6

For the choir director: A psalm of David, to be accompanied by an eight-stringed instrument.

[1]O LORD, do not rebuke me in your anger
   or discipline me in your rage.
[2]Have compassion on me, LORD, for I am weak.
   Heal me, LORD, for my body is in agony.
[3]I am sick at heart.
   How long, O LORD, until you restore me?

[4]Return, O LORD, and rescue me.
   Save me because of your unfailing love.
[5]For in death, who remembers you?
   Who can praise you from the grave?

[6]I am worn out from sobbing.
   Every night tears drench my bed;
   my pillow is wet from weeping.
[7]My vision is blurred by grief;
   my eyes are worn out because of all my enemies.

⁸Go away, all you who do evil,
     for the LORD has heard my crying.
⁹The LORD has heard my plea;
     the LORD will answer my prayer.
¹⁰May all my enemies be disgraced and terrified.
     May they suddenly turn back in shame.

PSALM 7

A psalm of David, which he sang to the LORD concerning Cush of the tribe of Benjamin.

¹I come to you for protection, O LORD my God.
     Save me from my persecutors—rescue me!
²If you don't, they will maul me like a lion,
     tearing me to pieces with no one to rescue me.

³O LORD my God, if I have done wrong
     or am guilty of injustice,
⁴if I have betrayed a friend
     or plundered my enemy without cause,
⁵then let my enemies capture me.
     Let them trample me into the ground.
     Let my honor be left in the dust.   *Interlude*

⁶Arise, O LORD, in anger!

    Stand up against the fury of my enemies!

    Wake up, my God, and bring justice!

⁷Gather the nations before you.

    Sit on your throne high above them.

⁸The LORD passes judgment on the nations.

    Declare me righteous, O LORD,

    for I am innocent, O Most High!

⁹End the wickedness of the ungodly,

    but help all those who obey you.

For you look deep within the mind and heart,

    O righteous God.

¹⁰God is my shield,

    saving those whose hearts are true and right.

¹¹God is a judge who is perfectly fair.

    He is angry with the wicked every day.

¹²If a person does not repent,

    God will sharpen his sword;

    he will bend and string his bow.

¹³He will prepare his deadly weapons

    and ignite his flaming arrows.

¹⁴The wicked conceive evil;

    they are pregnant with trouble

    and give birth to lies.

¹⁵They dig a pit to trap others
   and then fall into it themselves.
¹⁶They make trouble,
   but it backfires on them.
They plan violence for others,
   but it falls on their own heads.

¹⁷I will thank the LORD because he is just;
   I will sing praise to the name of the LORD Most High.

PSALM 8

*For the choir director: A psalm of David, to be accompanied by a
stringed instrument.*

¹O LORD, our Lord, the majesty of your name fills the
      earth!
   Your glory is higher than the heavens.

²You have taught children and nursing infants
   to give you praise.
They silence your enemies
   who were seeking revenge.

³When I look at the night sky and see the work of your
      fingers—
   the moon and the stars you have set in place—

⁴what are mortals that you should think of us,
>mere humans that you should care for us?
⁵For you made us only a little lower than God,
>and you crowned us with glory and honor.
⁶You put us in charge of everything you made,
>giving us authority over all things—
⁷the sheep and the cattle
>and all the wild animals,
⁸the birds in the sky, the fish in the sea,
>and everything that swims the ocean currents.

⁹O LORD, our Lord, the majesty of your name fills the earth!

PSALM 9

For the choir director: A psalm of David, to be sung to the tune "Death of the Son."

¹I will thank you, LORD, with all my heart;
>I will tell of all the marvelous things you have done.
²I will be filled with joy because of you.
>I will sing praises to your name, O Most High.

³My enemies turn away in retreat;
>they are overthrown and destroyed before you.
⁴For you have judged in my favor;
>from your throne, you have judged with fairness.

⁵You have rebuked the nations and destroyed the
        wicked;
    you have wiped out their names forever.
⁶My enemies have met their doom;
    their cities are perpetual ruins.
    Even the memory of their uprooted cities is lost.

⁷But the LORD reigns forever,
    executing judgment from his throne.
⁸He will judge the world with justice
    and rule the nations with fairness.

⁹The LORD is a shelter for the oppressed,
    a refuge in times of trouble.
¹⁰Those who know your name trust in you,
    for you, O LORD, have never abandoned anyone who
        searches for you.

¹¹Sing praises to the LORD who reigns in Jerusalem.
    Tell the world about his unforgettable deeds.
¹²For he who avenges murder cares for the helpless.
    He does not ignore those who cry to him for help.

¹³LORD, have mercy on me.
    See how I suffer at the hands of those who hate me.
    Snatch me back from the jaws of death.

¹⁴Save me, so I can praise you publicly at Jerusalem's gates,
  so I can rejoice that you have rescued me.

¹⁵The nations have fallen into the pit they dug for others.
  They have been caught in their own trap.
¹⁶The LORD is known for his justice.
  The wicked have trapped themselves in their own
    snares.   *Quiet Interlude*

¹⁷The wicked will go down to the grave.
  This is the fate of all the nations who ignore God.
¹⁸For the needy will not be forgotten forever;
  the hopes of the poor will not always be crushed.

¹⁹Arise, O LORD!
  Do not let mere mortals defy you!
  Let the nations be judged in your presence!
²⁰Make them tremble in fear, O LORD.
  Let them know they are merely human.   *Interlude*

PSALM 10

¹O LORD, why do you stand so far away?
  Why do you hide when I need you the most?
²Proud and wicked people viciously oppress the poor.
  Let them be caught in the evil they plan for others.

³For they brag about their evil desires;

    they praise the greedy and curse the LORD.

⁴These wicked people are too proud to seek God.

    They seem to think that God is dead.

⁵Yet they succeed in everything they do.

    They do not see your punishment awaiting them.

    They pour scorn on all their enemies.

⁶They say to themselves, "Nothing bad will ever happen to us!

    We will be free of trouble forever!"

⁷Their mouths are full of cursing, lies, and threats.

    Trouble and evil are on the tips of their tongues.

⁸They lurk in dark alleys,

    murdering the innocent who pass by.

They are always searching

    for some helpless victim.

⁹Like lions they crouch silently,

    waiting to pounce on the helpless.

Like hunters they capture their victims

    and drag them away in nets.

¹⁰The helpless are overwhelmed and collapse;

    they fall beneath the strength of the wicked.

¹¹The wicked say to themselves, "God isn't watching!

    He will never notice!"

¹²Arise, O LORD!

> Punish the wicked, O God!

> Do not forget the helpless!

¹³Why do the wicked get away with cursing God?

> How can they think, "God will never call us to account"?

¹⁴But you do see the trouble and grief they cause.

> You take note of it and punish them.

The helpless put their trust in you.

> You are the defender of orphans.

¹⁵Break the arms of these wicked, evil people!

> Go after them until the last one is destroyed!

¹⁶The LORD is king forever and ever!

> Let those who worship other gods be swept from the land.

¹⁷LORD, you know the hopes of the helpless.

> Surely you will listen to their cries and comfort them.

¹⁸You will bring justice to the orphans and the oppressed,

> so people can no longer terrify them.

PROVERBS 2

My child, listen to me and treasure my instructions. ²Tune your ears to wisdom, and concentrate on understanding. ³Cry out for insight and understanding. ⁴Search for them as you would for lost money or hidden treasure. ⁵Then you will understand what it means to fear the LORD, and you will gain knowledge of God. ⁶For the LORD grants wisdom! From his mouth come knowledge and understanding. ⁷He grants a treasure of good sense to the godly. He is their shield, protecting those who walk with integrity. ⁸He guards the paths of justice and protects those who are faithful to him.

⁹Then you will understand what is right, just, and fair, and you will know how to find the right course of action every time. ¹⁰For wisdom will enter your heart, and knowledge will fill you with joy. ¹¹Wise planning will watch over you. Understanding will keep you safe.

¹²Wisdom will save you from evil people, from those whose speech is corrupt. ¹³These people turn from right ways to walk down dark and evil paths. ¹⁴They rejoice in doing wrong, and they enjoy evil as it turns things upside down. ¹⁵What they do is crooked, and their ways are wrong.

¹⁶Wisdom will save you from the immoral woman, from the flattery of the adulterous woman. ¹⁷She has abandoned her husband and ignores the covenant she made before God. ¹⁸Entering her house leads to death; it is the road to hell. ¹⁹The man who visits her is doomed. He will never reach the paths of life.

²⁰Follow the steps of good men instead, and stay on the paths of the righteous. ²¹For only the upright will live in the land, and those who have integrity will remain in it. ²²But the wicked will be removed from the land, and the treacherous will be destroyed.

PSALM 11

For the choir director: A psalm of David.

¹I trust in the LORD for protection.
     So why do you say to me,
"Fly to the mountains for safety!
²   The wicked are stringing their bows
          and setting their arrows in the bowstrings.
     They shoot from the shadows at those who do right.
³The foundations of law and order have collapsed.
     What can the righteous do?"

⁴But the LORD is in his holy Temple;
     the LORD still rules from heaven.
He watches everything closely,
          examining everyone on earth.
⁵The LORD examines both the righteous and the wicked.
     He hates everyone who loves violence.
⁶He rains down blazing coals on the wicked,
     punishing them with burning sulfur and scorching winds.

⁷For the LORD is righteous, and he loves justice.
Those who do what is right will see his face.

PSALM 12

*For the choir director: A psalm of David, to be accompanied by an
eight-stringed instrument.*

¹Help, O LORD, for the godly are fast disappearing!
The faithful have vanished from the earth!
²Neighbors lie to each other,
speaking with flattering lips and insincere hearts.
³May the LORD bring their flattery to an end
and silence their proud tongues.
⁴They say, "We will lie to our hearts' content.
Our lips are our own—who can stop us?"

⁵The LORD replies, "I have seen violence done to the
helpless,
and I have heard the groans of the poor.
Now I will rise up to rescue them,
as they have longed for me to do."
⁶The LORD's promises are pure,
like silver refined in a furnace,
purified seven times over.

⁷Therefore, LORD, we know you will protect the oppressed,
　　preserving them forever from this lying generation,
⁸even though the wicked strut about,
　　and evil is praised throughout the land.

PSALM 13

For the choir director: A psalm of David.

¹O LORD, how long will you forget me? Forever?
　　How long will you look the other way?
²How long must I struggle with anguish in my soul,
　　with sorrow in my heart every day?
　　How long will my enemy have the upper hand?

³Turn and answer me, O LORD my God!
　　Restore the light to my eyes, or I will die.
⁴Don't let my enemies gloat, saying, "We have defeated
　　　him!"
　　Don't let them rejoice at my downfall.

⁵But I trust in your unfailing love.
　　I will rejoice because you have rescued me.
⁶I will sing to the LORD
　　because he has been so good to me.

PSALM 14

For the choir director: A psalm of David.

¹Only fools say in their hearts,
    "There is no God."
They are corrupt, and their actions are evil;
    no one does good!

²The LORD looks down from heaven
    on the entire human race;
he looks to see if there is even one with real
        understanding,
    one who seeks for God.
³But no, all have turned away from God;
    all have become corrupt.
No one does good,
    not even one!

⁴Will those who do evil never learn?
    They eat up my people like bread;
    they wouldn't think of praying to the LORD.
⁵Terror will grip them,
    for God is with those who obey him.
⁶The wicked frustrate the plans of the oppressed,
    but the LORD will protect his people.

⁷Oh, that salvation would come from Mount Zion to
      rescue Israel!
    For when the LORD restores his people,
    Jacob will shout with joy, and Israel will rejoice.

PSALM 15

A psalm of David.

¹Who may worship in your sanctuary, LORD?
    Who may enter your presence on your holy hill?

²Those who lead blameless lives
    and do what is right,
    speaking the truth from sincere hearts.
³Those who refuse to slander others
    or harm their neighbors
    or speak evil of their friends.
⁴Those who despise persistent sinners,
    and honor the faithful followers of the LORD
    and keep their promises even when it hurts.
⁵Those who do not charge interest on the money they lend,
    and who refuse to accept bribes to testify against the
      innocent.

Such people will stand firm forever.

My child, never forget the things I have taught you. Store my commands in your heart, [2]for they will give you a long and satisfying life. [3]Never let loyalty and kindness get away from you! Wear them like a necklace; write them deep within your heart. [4]Then you will find favor with both God and people, and you will gain a good reputation.

[5]Trust in the LORD with all your heart; do not depend on your own understanding. [6]Seek his will in all you do, and he will direct your paths.

[7]Don't be impressed with your own wisdom. Instead, fear the LORD and turn your back on evil. [8]Then you will gain renewed health and vitality.

[9]Honor the LORD with your wealth and with the best part of everything your land produces. [10]Then he will fill your barns with grain, and your vats will overflow with the finest wine.

[11]My child, don't ignore it when the LORD disciplines you, and don't be discouraged when he corrects you. [12]For the LORD corrects those he loves, just as a father corrects a child in whom he delights.

[13]Happy is the person who finds wisdom and gains understanding. [14]For the profit of wisdom is better than silver, and her wages are better than gold. [15]Wisdom is

more precious than rubies; nothing you desire can compare with her. ¹⁶She offers you life in her right hand, and riches and honor in her left. ¹⁷She will guide you down delightful paths; all her ways are satisfying. ¹⁸Wisdom is a tree of life to those who embrace her; happy are those who hold her tightly.

¹⁹By wisdom the LORD founded the earth; by understanding he established the heavens. ²⁰By his knowledge the deep fountains of the earth burst forth, and the clouds poured down rain.

²¹My child, don't lose sight of good planning and insight. Hang on to them, ²²for they fill you with life and bring you honor and respect. ²³They keep you safe on your way and keep your feet from stumbling. ²⁴You can lie down without fear and enjoy pleasant dreams. ²⁵You need not be afraid of disaster or the destruction that comes upon the wicked, ²⁶for the LORD is your security. He will keep your foot from being caught in a trap.

²⁷Do not withhold good from those who deserve it when it's in your power to help them. ²⁸If you can help your neighbor now, don't say, "Come back tomorrow, and then I'll help you."

²⁹Do not plot against your neighbors, for they trust

you. ³⁰Don't make accusations against someone who hasn't wronged you.

³¹Do not envy violent people; don't copy their ways.
³²Such wicked people are an abomination to the LORD, but he offers his friendship to the godly.

³³The curse of the LORD is on the house of the wicked, but his blessing is on the home of the upright.

³⁴The LORD mocks at mockers, but he shows favor to the humble.

³⁵The wise inherit honor, but fools are put to shame!

DAY FOUR

Psalm 16

A psalm of David.

¹Keep me safe, O God,
  for I have come to you for refuge.

²I said to the LORD, "You are my Master!
  All the good things I have are from you."
³The godly people in the land
  are my true heroes!
  I take pleasure in them!
⁴Those who chase after other gods will be filled with
    sorrow.
  I will not take part in their sacrifices
  or even speak the names of their gods.

⁵LORD, you alone are my inheritance, my cup of blessing.
  You guard all that is mine.
⁶The land you have given me is a pleasant land.
  What a wonderful inheritance!

⁷I will bless the LORD who guides me;
  even at night my heart instructs me.
⁸I know the LORD is always with me.
  I will not be shaken, for he is right beside me.

⁹No wonder my heart is filled with joy,
  and my mouth shouts his praises!
  My body rests in safety.
¹⁰For you will not leave my soul among the dead
  or allow your godly one to rot in the grave.
¹¹You will show me the way of life,
  granting me the joy of your presence
  and the pleasures of living with you forever.

PSALM 17

A prayer of David.

¹O LORD, hear my plea for justice.
  Listen to my cry for help.
Pay attention to my prayer,
  for it comes from an honest heart.
²Declare me innocent,
  for you know those who do right.

³You have tested my thoughts and examined my heart in
    the night.

You have scrutinized me and found nothing amiss,
   for I am determined not to sin in what I say.
⁴I have followed your commands,
      which have kept me from going along with cruel and
         evil people.
⁵My steps have stayed on your path;
      I have not wavered from following you.

⁶I am praying to you because I know you will answer,
         O God.
      Bend down and listen as I pray.
⁷Show me your unfailing love in wonderful ways.
      You save with your strength
      those who seek refuge from their enemies.
⁸Guard me as the apple of your eye.
      Hide me in the shadow of your wings.
⁹Protect me from wicked people who attack me,
      from murderous enemies who surround me.

¹⁰They are without pity.
      Listen to their boasting.
¹¹They track me down, surround me,
      and throw me to the ground.
¹²They are like hungry lions, eager to tear me apart—
      like young lions in hiding, waiting for their chance.

¹³Arise, O Lord!

> Stand against them and bring them to their knees!

> Rescue me from the wicked with your sword!

¹⁴Save me by your mighty hand, O Lord,

> from those whose only concern is earthly gain.

May they have their punishment in full.

> May their children inherit more of the same,

> and may the judgment continue to their children's
> children.

¹⁵But because I have done what is right, I will see you.

> When I awake, I will be fully satisfied,

> for I will see you face to face.

PSALM 18

For the choir director: A psalm of David, the servant of the Lord. He sang this song to the Lord on the day the Lord rescued him from all his enemies and from Saul.

¹I love you, Lord; you are my strength.

²The Lord is my rock, my fortress, and my savior;

> my God is my rock, in whom I find protection.

> He is my shield, the strength of my salvation, and my
> stronghold.

³I will call on the Lord, who is worthy of praise,

> for he saves me from my enemies.

⁴The ropes of death surrounded me;
  the floods of destruction swept over me.
⁵The grave wrapped its ropes around me;
  death itself stared me in the face.
⁶But in my distress I cried out to the LORD;
  yes, I prayed to my God for help.
He heard me from his sanctuary;
  my cry reached his ears.

⁷Then the earth quaked and trembled;
  the foundations of the mountains shook;
  they quaked because of his anger.
⁸Smoke poured from his nostrils;
  fierce flames leaped from his mouth;
  glowing coals flamed forth from him.
⁹He opened the heavens and came down;
  dark storm clouds were beneath his feet.
¹⁰Mounted on a mighty angel, he flew,
  soaring on the wings of the wind.
¹¹He shrouded himself in darkness,
  veiling his approach with dense rain clouds.
¹²The brilliance of his presence broke through the clouds,
  raining down hail and burning coals.
¹³The LORD thundered from heaven;
  the Most High gave a mighty shout.

¹⁴He shot his arrows and scattered his enemies;

    his lightning flashed, and they were greatly confused.

¹⁵Then at your command, O LORD,

    at the blast of your breath,

the bottom of the sea could be seen,

    and the foundations of the earth were laid bare.

¹⁶He reached down from heaven and rescued me;

    he drew me out of deep waters.

¹⁷He delivered me from my powerful enemies,

    from those who hated me and were too strong for me.

¹⁸They attacked me at a moment when I was weakest,

    but the LORD upheld me.

¹⁹He led me to a place of safety;

    he rescued me because he delights in me.

²⁰The LORD rewarded me for doing right;

    he compensated me because of my innocence.

²¹For I have kept the ways of the LORD;

    I have not turned from my God to follow evil.

²²For all his laws are constantly before me;

    I have never abandoned his principles.

²³I am blameless before God;

    I have kept myself from sin.

²⁴The LORD rewarded me for doing right,

    because of the innocence of my hands in his sight.

²⁵To the faithful you show yourself faithful;

to those with integrity you show integrity.

²⁶To the pure you show yourself pure,

but to the wicked you show yourself hostile.

²⁷You rescue those who are humble,

but you humiliate the proud.

²⁸LORD, you have brought light to my life;

my God, you light up my darkness.

²⁹In your strength I can crush an army;

with my God I can scale any wall.

³⁰As for God, his way is perfect.

All the LORD's promises prove true.

He is a shield for all who look to him for protection.

³¹For who is God except the LORD?

Who but our God is a solid rock?

³²God arms me with strength;

he has made my way safe.

³³He makes me as surefooted as a deer,

leading me safely along the mountain heights.

³⁴He prepares me for battle;

he strengthens me to draw a bow of bronze.

³⁵You have given me the shield of your salvation.

Your right hand supports me;

your gentleness has made me great.

³⁶You have made a wide path for my feet
    to keep them from slipping.

³⁷I chased my enemies and caught them;
    I did not stop until they were conquered.
³⁸I struck them down so they could not get up;
    they fell beneath my feet.
³⁹You have armed me with strength for the battle;
    you have subdued my enemies under my feet.
⁴⁰You made them turn and run;
    I have destroyed all who hated me.
⁴¹They called for help, but no one came to rescue them.
    They cried to the LORD, but he refused to answer them.
⁴²I ground them as fine as dust carried by the wind.
    I swept them into the gutter like dirt.

⁴³You gave me victory over my accusers.
    You appointed me as the ruler over nations;
    people I don't even know now serve me.
⁴⁴As soon as they hear of me, they submit;
    foreigners cringe before me.
⁴⁵They all lose their courage
    and come trembling from their strongholds.

⁴⁶The LORD lives! Blessed be my rock!
    May the God of my salvation be exalted!

⁴⁷He is the God who pays back those who harm me;
     he subdues the nations under me
⁴⁸   and rescues me from my enemies.
You hold me safe beyond the reach of my enemies;
     you save me from violent opponents.
⁴⁹For this, O LORD, I will praise you among the nations;
     I will sing joyfully to your name.
⁵⁰You give great victories to your king;
     you show unfailing love to your anointed,
     to David and all his descendants forever.

PSALM 19

For the choir director: A psalm of David.

¹The heavens tell of the glory of God.
     The skies display his marvelous craftsmanship.
²Day after day they continue to speak;
     night after night they make him known.
³They speak without a sound or a word;
     their voice is silent in the skies;
⁴yet their message has gone out to all the earth,
     and their words to all the world.

The sun lives in the heavens
     where God placed it.

[5]It bursts forth like a radiant bridegroom
     after his wedding.
It rejoices like a great athlete
     eager to run the race.
[6]The sun rises at one end of the heavens
     and follows its course to the other end.
     Nothing can hide from its heat.

[7]The law of the LORD is perfect,
     reviving the soul.
The decrees of the LORD are trustworthy,
     making wise the simple.
[8]The commandments of the LORD are right,
     bringing joy to the heart.
The commands of the LORD are clear,
     giving insight to life.
[9]Reverence for the LORD is pure,
     lasting forever.
The laws of the LORD are true;
     each one is fair.
[10]They are more desirable than gold,
     even the finest gold.
They are sweeter than honey,
     even honey dripping from the comb.

[11]They are a warning to those who hear them;
　　　there is great reward for those who obey them.

[12]How can I know all the sins lurking in my heart?
　　　Cleanse me from these hidden faults.
[13]Keep me from deliberate sins!
　　　Don't let them control me.
Then I will be free of guilt
　　　and innocent of great sin.

[14]May the words of my mouth and the thoughts of my heart
　　　be pleasing to you,
　　　O LORD, my rock and my redeemer.

PSALM 20

For the choir director: A psalm of David.

[1]In times of trouble, may the LORD respond to your cry.
　　　May the God of Israel keep you safe from all harm.
[2]May he send you help from his sanctuary
　　　and strengthen you from Jerusalem.
[3]May he remember all your gifts
　　　and look favorably on your burnt offerings.　　*Interlude*

[4]May he grant your heart's desire
　　　and fulfill all your plans.

⁵May we shout for joy when we hear of your victory,
  flying banners to honor our God.
May the LORD answer all your prayers.

⁶Now I know that the LORD saves his anointed king.
  He will answer him from his holy heaven
  and rescue him by his great power.
⁷Some nations boast of their armies and weapons,
  but we boast in the LORD our God.
⁸Those nations will fall down and collapse,
  but we will rise up and stand firm.

⁹Give victory to our king, O LORD!
  Respond to our cry for help.

PROVERBS 4

My children, listen to me. Listen to your father's instruction.
Pay attention and grow wise, ²for I am giving you good guidance. Don't turn away from my teaching. ³For I, too, was
once my father's son, tenderly loved by my mother as an only
child.

⁴My father told me, "Take my words to heart. Follow
my instructions and you will live. ⁵Learn to be wise, and
develop good judgment. Don't forget or turn away from
my words. ⁶Don't turn your back on wisdom, for she will

protect you. Love her, and she will guard you. ⁷Getting wisdom is the most important thing you can do! And whatever else you do, get good judgment. ⁸If you prize wisdom, she will exalt you. Embrace her and she will honor you. ⁹She will place a lovely wreath on your head; she will present you with a beautiful crown."

¹⁰My child, listen to me and do as I say, and you will have a long, good life. ¹¹I will teach you wisdom's ways and lead you in straight paths. ¹²If you live a life guided by wisdom, you won't limp or stumble as you run. ¹³Carry out my instructions; don't forsake them. Guard them, for they will lead you to a fulfilled life.

¹⁴Do not do as the wicked do or follow the path of evildoers. ¹⁵Avoid their haunts. Turn away and go somewhere else, ¹⁶for evil people cannot sleep until they have done their evil deed for the day. They cannot rest unless they have caused someone to stumble. ¹⁷They eat wickedness and drink violence!

¹⁸The way of the righteous is like the first gleam of dawn, which shines ever brighter until the full light of day. ¹⁹But the way of the wicked is like complete darkness. Those who follow it have no idea what they are stumbling over.

²⁰Pay attention, my child, to what I say. Listen

carefully. ²¹Don't lose sight of my words. Let them penetrate deep within your heart, ²²for they bring life and radiant health to anyone who discovers their meaning.

²³Above all else, guard your heart, for it affects everything you do.

²⁴Avoid all perverse talk; stay far from corrupt speech.

²⁵Look straight ahead, and fix your eyes on what lies before you. ²⁶Mark out a straight path for your feet; then stick to the path and stay safe. ²⁷Don't get sidetracked; keep your feet from following evil.

DAY FIVE

PSALM 21

For the choir director: A psalm of David.

¹How the king rejoices in your strength, O LORD!
  He shouts with joy because of your victory.
²For you have given him his heart's desire;
  you have held back nothing that he requested. *Interlude*

³You welcomed him back with success and prosperity.
  You placed a crown of finest gold on his head.
⁴He asked you to preserve his life,
  and you have granted his request.
  The days of his life stretch on forever.
⁵Your victory brings him great honor,
  and you have clothed him with splendor and majesty.
⁶You have endowed him with eternal blessings.
  You have given him the joy of being in your presence.
⁷For the king trusts in the LORD.
  The unfailing love of the Most High will keep him
    from stumbling.

⁸You will capture all your enemies.
    Your strong right hand will seize all those who hate you.
⁹You will destroy them as in a flaming furnace
    when you appear.
The LORD will consume them in his anger;
    fire will devour them.
¹⁰You will wipe their children from the face of the earth;
    they will never have descendants.
¹¹Although they plot against you,
    their evil schemes will never succeed.
¹²For they will turn and run
    when they see your arrows aimed at them.

¹³We praise you, LORD, for all your glorious power.
    With music and singing we celebrate your mighty acts.

PSALM 22

For the choir director: A psalm of David, to be sung to the tune "Doe of the Dawn."

¹My God, my God! Why have you forsaken me?
    Why do you remain so distant?
    Why do you ignore my cries for help?
²Every day I call to you, my God, but you do not answer.
    Every night you hear my voice, but I find no relief.

³Yet you are holy.

> The praises of Israel surround your throne.

⁴Our ancestors trusted in you,

> and you rescued them.

⁵You heard their cries for help and saved them.

> They put their trust in you and were never
> > disappointed.

⁶But I am a worm and not a man.

> I am scorned and despised by all!

⁷Everyone who sees me mocks me.

> They sneer and shake their heads, saying,

⁸"Is this the one who relies on the LORD?

> Then let the LORD save him!

If the LORD loves him so much,

> let the LORD rescue him!"

⁹Yet you brought me safely from my mother's womb

> and led me to trust you when I was a nursing infant.

¹⁰I was thrust upon you at my birth.

> You have been my God from the moment I was
> > born.

¹¹Do not stay so far from me,

> for trouble is near,
> and no one else can help me.

¹²My enemies surround me like a herd of bulls;
    fierce bulls of Bashan have hemmed me in!
¹³Like roaring lions attacking their prey,
    they come at me with open mouths.
¹⁴My life is poured out like water,
    and all my bones are out of joint.
My heart is like wax,
    melting within me.
¹⁵My strength has dried up like sunbaked clay.
    My tongue sticks to the roof of my mouth.
    You have laid me in the dust and left me for dead.

¹⁶My enemies surround me like a pack of dogs;
    an evil gang closes in on me.
    They have pierced my hands and feet.
¹⁷I can count every bone in my body.
    My enemies stare at me and gloat.
¹⁸They divide my clothes among themselves
    and throw dice for my garments.

¹⁹O Lᴏʀᴅ, do not stay away!
    You are my strength; come quickly to my aid!
²⁰Rescue me from a violent death;
    spare my precious life from these dogs.

²¹Snatch me from the lions' jaws,
  and from the horns of these wild oxen.

²²Then I will declare the wonder of your name to my
      brothers and sisters.
  I will praise you among all your people.
²³Praise the LORD, all you who fear him!
  Honor him, all you descendants of Jacob!
  Show him reverence, all you descendants of Israel!
²⁴For he has not ignored the suffering of the needy.
  He has not turned and walked away.
  He has listened to their cries for help.

²⁵I will praise you among all the people;
  I will fulfill my vows in the presence of those who
      worship you.
²⁶The poor will eat and be satisfied.
  All who seek the LORD will praise him.
  Their hearts will rejoice with everlasting joy.
²⁷The whole earth will acknowledge the LORD and return
      to him.
  People from every nation will bow down before him.
²⁸For the LORD is king!
  He rules all the nations.

²⁹Let the rich of the earth feast and worship.

> Let all mortals—those born to die—bow down in his
> > presence.

³⁰Future generations will also serve him.

> Our children will hear about the wonders of the Lord.

³¹His righteous acts will be told to those yet unborn.

> They will hear about everything he has done.

PSALM 23

A psalm of David.

¹The LORD is my shepherd;

> I have everything I need.

²He lets me rest in green meadows;

> he leads me beside peaceful streams.

³   He renews my strength.

He guides me along right paths,

> bringing honor to his name.

⁴Even when I walk

> through the dark valley of death,

I will not be afraid,

> for you are close beside me.

Your rod and your staff

> protect and comfort me.

⁵You prepare a feast for me
    in the presence of my enemies.
You welcome me as a guest,
    anointing my head with oil.
    My cup overflows with blessings.
⁶Surely your goodness and unfailing love will pursue me
    all the days of my life,
and I will live in the house of the LORD
    forever.

PSALM 24

A psalm of David.

¹The earth is the LORD's, and everything in it.
    The world and all its people belong to him.
²For he laid the earth's foundation on the seas
    and built it on the ocean depths.

³Who may climb the mountain of the LORD?
    Who may stand in his holy place?
⁴Only those whose hands and hearts are pure,
    who do not worship idols
    and never tell lies.
⁵They will receive the LORD's blessing
    and have right standing with God their savior.

⁶They alone may enter God's presence
　　　and worship the God of Israel.　　　　　　　　*Interlude*

⁷Open up, ancient gates!
　　　Open up, ancient doors,
　　　and let the King of glory enter.
⁸Who is the King of glory?
　　　The LORD, strong and mighty,
　　　the LORD, invincible in battle.
⁹Open up, ancient gates!
　　　Open up, ancient doors,
　　　and let the King of glory enter.
¹⁰Who is the King of glory?
　　　The LORD Almighty—
　　　he is the King of glory.　　　　　　　　　　*Interlude*

PSALM 25

A psalm of David.

¹To you, O LORD, I lift up my soul.
²　　I trust in you, my God!
Do not let me be disgraced,
　　　or let my enemies rejoice in my defeat.
³No one who trusts in you will ever be disgraced,
　　　but disgrace comes to those who try to deceive others.

⁴Show me the path where I should walk, O Lord;
    point out the right road for me to follow.
⁵Lead me by your truth and teach me,
    for you are the God who saves me.
    All day long I put my hope in you.

⁶Remember, O Lord, your unfailing love and
        compassion,
    which you have shown from long ages past.
⁷Forgive the rebellious sins of my youth;
    look instead through the eyes of your unfailing love,
    for you are merciful, O Lord.

⁸The Lord is good and does what is right;
    he shows the proper path to those who go astray.
⁹He leads the humble in what is right,
    teaching them his way.
¹⁰The Lord leads with unfailing love and faithfulness
    all those who keep his covenant and obey his decrees.

¹¹For the honor of your name, O Lord,
    forgive my many, many sins.
¹²Who are those who fear the Lord?
    He will show them the path they should choose.
¹³They will live in prosperity,
    and their children will inherit the Promised Land.

¹⁴Friendship with the LORD is reserved for those who fear him.

With them he shares the secrets of his covenant.

¹⁵My eyes are always looking to the LORD for help,

for he alone can rescue me from the traps of my enemies.

¹⁶Turn to me and have mercy on me,

for I am alone and in deep distress.

¹⁷My problems go from bad to worse.

Oh, save me from them all!

¹⁸Feel my pain and see my trouble.

Forgive all my sins.

¹⁹See how many enemies I have,

and how viciously they hate me!

²⁰Protect me! Rescue my life from them!

Do not let me be disgraced, for I trust in you.

²¹May integrity and honesty protect me,

for I put my hope in you.

²²O God, ransom Israel

from all its troubles.

PROVERBS 5

My son, pay attention to my wisdom; listen carefully to my wise counsel. ²Then you will learn to be discreet and will store up knowledge.

³The lips of an immoral woman are as sweet as honey, and her mouth is smoother than oil. ⁴But the result is as bitter as poison, sharp as a double-edged sword. ⁵Her feet go down to death; her steps lead straight to the grave. ⁶For she does not care about the path to life. She staggers down a crooked trail and doesn't even realize where it leads.

⁷So now, my sons, listen to me. Never stray from what I am about to say: ⁸Run from her! Don't go near the door of her house! ⁹If you do, you will lose your honor and hand over to merciless people everything you have achieved in life. ¹⁰Strangers will obtain your wealth, and someone else will enjoy the fruit of your labor. ¹¹Afterward you will groan in anguish when disease consumes your body, ¹²and you will say, "How I hated discipline! If only I had not demanded my own way! ¹³Oh, why didn't I listen to my teachers? Why didn't I pay attention to those who gave me instruction? ¹⁴I have come to the brink of utter ruin, and now I must face public disgrace."

¹⁵Drink water from your own well—share your love only with your wife. ¹⁶Why spill the water of your springs in public, having sex with just anyone? ¹⁷You should reserve it for yourselves. Don't share it with strangers.

¹⁸Let your wife be a fountain of blessing for you. Rejoice in the wife of your youth. ¹⁹She is a loving doe, a

graceful deer. Let her breasts satisfy you always. May you always be captivated by her love. [20]Why be captivated, my son, with an immoral woman, or embrace the breasts of an adulterous woman?

[21]For the LORD sees clearly what a man does, examining every path he takes. [22]An evil man is held captive by his own sins; they are ropes that catch and hold him. [23]He will die for lack of self-control; he will be lost because of his incredible folly.

DAY SIX

PSALM 26

A psalm of David.

¹Declare me innocent, O LORD,
   for I have acted with integrity;
   I have trusted in the LORD without wavering.
²Put me on trial, LORD, and cross-examine me.
   Test my motives and affections.
³For I am constantly aware of your unfailing love,
   and I have lived according to your truth.

⁴I do not spend time with liars
   or go along with hypocrites.
⁵I hate the gatherings of those who do evil,
   and I refuse to join in with the wicked.

⁶I wash my hands to declare my innocence.
   I come to your altar, O LORD,
⁷singing a song of thanksgiving
   and telling of all your miracles.

⁸I love your sanctuary, LORD,
the place where your glory shines.

⁹Don't let me suffer the fate of sinners.
Don't condemn me along with murderers.
¹⁰Their hands are dirty with wicked schemes,
and they constantly take bribes.

¹¹But I am not like that; I do what is right.
So in your mercy, save me.
¹²I have taken a stand,
and I will publicly praise the LORD.

PSALM 27

A psalm of David.

¹The LORD is my light and my salvation—
so why should I be afraid?
The LORD protects me from danger—
so why should I tremble?

²When evil people come to destroy me,
when my enemies and foes attack me,
they will stumble and fall.
³Though a mighty army surrounds me,
my heart will know no fear.

Even if they attack me,
  I remain confident.

⁴The one thing I ask of the LORD—
  the thing I seek most—
is to live in the house of the LORD all the days of my life,
  delighting in the LORD's perfections
  and meditating in his Temple.
⁵For he will conceal me there when troubles come;
  he will hide me in his sanctuary.
  He will place me out of reach on a high rock.
⁶Then I will hold my head high,
  above my enemies who surround me.
At his Tabernacle I will offer sacrifices with shouts of joy,
  singing and praising the LORD with music.

⁷Listen to my pleading, O LORD.
  Be merciful and answer me!
⁸My heart has heard you say, "Come and talk with me."
  And my heart responds, "LORD, I am coming."
⁹Do not hide yourself from me.
  Do not reject your servant in anger.
  You have always been my helper.
Don't leave me now; don't abandon me,
  O God of my salvation!

¹⁰Even if my father and mother abandon me,
the LORD will hold me close.

¹¹Teach me how to live, O LORD.
Lead me along the path of honesty,
for my enemies are waiting for me to fall.
¹²Do not let me fall into their hands.
For they accuse me of things I've never done
and breathe out violence against me.
¹³Yet I am confident that I will see the LORD's goodness
while I am here in the land of the living.

¹⁴Wait patiently for the LORD.
Be brave and courageous.
Yes, wait patiently for the LORD.

PSALM 28

A psalm of David.

¹O LORD, you are my rock of safety.
Please help me; don't refuse to answer me.
For if you are silent,
I might as well give up and die.
²Listen to my prayer for mercy
as I cry out to you for help,
as I lift my hands toward your holy sanctuary.

³Don't drag me away with the wicked—
  with those who do evil—
those who speak friendly words to their neighbors
  while planning evil in their hearts.
⁴Give them the punishment they so richly deserve!
  Measure it out in proportion to their wickedness.
Pay them back for all their evil deeds!
  Give them a taste of what they have done to others.
⁵They care nothing for what the LORD has done
  or for what his hands have made.
So he will tear them down like old buildings,
  and they will never be rebuilt!

⁶Praise the LORD!
  For he has heard my cry for mercy.
⁷The LORD is my strength, my shield from every danger.
  I trust in him with all my heart.
He helps me, and my heart is filled with joy.
  I burst out in songs of thanksgiving.

⁸The LORD protects his people
  and gives victory to his anointed king.
⁹Save your people!
  Bless Israel, your special possession!
Lead them like a shepherd,
  and carry them forever in your arms.

A psalm of David.

¹Give honor to the LORD, you angels;
  give honor to the LORD for his glory and strength.
²Give honor to the LORD for the glory of his name.
  Worship the LORD in the splendor of his holiness.

³The voice of the LORD echoes above the sea.
  The God of glory thunders.
  The LORD thunders over the mighty sea.
⁴The voice of the LORD is powerful;
  the voice of the LORD is full of majesty.
⁵The voice of the LORD splits the mighty cedars;
  the LORD shatters the cedars of Lebanon.
⁶He makes Lebanon's mountains skip like a calf
  and Mount Hermon to leap like a young bull.
⁷The voice of the LORD strikes with lightning bolts.
⁸The voice of the LORD makes the desert quake;
  the LORD shakes the desert of Kadesh.
⁹The voice of the LORD twists mighty oaks
  and strips the forests bare.
In his Temple everyone shouts, "Glory!"

¹⁰The LORD rules over the floodwaters.

The LORD reigns as king forever.

The LORD reigns as king forever.
¹¹The LORD gives his people strength.
The LORD blesses them with peace.

PSALM 30

A psalm of David, sung at the dedication of the Temple.

¹I will praise you, LORD, for you have rescued me.
You refused to let my enemies triumph over me.
²O LORD my God, I cried out to you for help,
and you restored my health.
³You brought me up from the grave, O LORD.
You kept me from falling into the pit of death.

⁴Sing to the LORD, all you godly ones!
Praise his holy name.
⁵His anger lasts for a moment,
but his favor lasts a lifetime!
Weeping may go on all night,
but joy comes with the morning.

⁶When I was prosperous I said,
"Nothing can stop me now!"
⁷Your favor, O LORD, made me as secure as a mountain.
Then you turned away from me, and I was shattered.

[8]I cried out to you, O LORD.

I begged the Lord for mercy, saying,

[9]"What will you gain if I die,

if I sink down into the grave?

Can my dust praise you from the grave?

Can it tell the world of your faithfulness?

[10]Hear me, LORD, and have mercy on me.

Help me, O LORD."

[11]You have turned my mourning into joyful dancing.

You have taken away my clothes of mourning and

clothed me with joy,

[12]that I might sing praises to you and not be silent.

O LORD my God, I will give you thanks forever!

PROVERBS 6

My child, if you co-sign a loan for a friend or guarantee the debt of someone you hardly know—[2]if you have trapped yourself by your agreement and are caught by what you said—[3]quick, get out of it if you possibly can! You have placed yourself at your friend's mercy. Now swallow your pride; go and beg to have your name erased. [4]Don't put it off. Do it now! Don't rest until you do. [5]Save yourself like a deer escaping from a hunter, like a bird fleeing from a net.

⁶Take a lesson from the ants, you lazybones. Learn from their ways and be wise! ⁷Even though they have no prince, governor, or ruler to make them work, ⁸they labor hard all summer, gathering food for the winter. ⁹But you, lazybones, how long will you sleep? When will you wake up? I want you to learn this lesson: ¹⁰A little extra sleep, a little more slumber, a little folding of the hands to rest— ¹¹and poverty will pounce on you like a bandit; scarcity will attack you like an armed robber.

¹²Here is a description of worthless and wicked people: They are constant liars, ¹³signaling their true intentions to their friends by making signs with their eyes and feet and fingers. ¹⁴Their perverted hearts plot evil. They stir up trouble constantly. ¹⁵But they will be destroyed suddenly, broken beyond all hope of healing.

¹⁶There are six things the LORD hates—no, seven things he detests:
¹⁷ haughty eyes,
    a lying tongue,
    hands that kill the innocent,
¹⁸ a heart that plots evil,
    feet that race to do wrong,
¹⁹ a false witness who pours out lies,
    a person who sows discord among brothers.

²⁰My son, obey your father's commands, and don't neglect your mother's teaching. ²¹Keep their words always in your heart. Tie them around your neck. ²²Wherever you walk, their counsel can lead you. When you sleep, they will protect you. When you wake up in the morning, they will advise you. ²³For these commands and this teaching are a lamp to light the way ahead of you. The correction of discipline is the way to life.

²⁴These commands and this teaching will keep you from the immoral woman, from the smooth tongue of an adulterous woman. ²⁵Don't lust for her beauty. Don't let her coyness seduce you. ²⁶For a prostitute will bring you to poverty, and sleeping with another man's wife may cost you your very life. ²⁷Can a man scoop fire into his lap and not be burned? ²⁸Can he walk on hot coals and not blister his feet? ²⁹So it is with the man who sleeps with another man's wife. He who embraces her will not go unpunished.

³⁰Excuses might be found for a thief who steals because he is starving. ³¹But if he is caught, he will be fined seven times as much as he stole, even if it means selling everything in his house to pay it back.

³²But the man who commits adultery is an utter fool, for he destroys his own soul. ³³Wounds and constant

disgrace are his lot. His shame will never be erased. ³⁴For the woman's husband will be furious in his jealousy, and he will have no mercy in his day of vengeance. ³⁵There is no compensation or bribe that will satisfy him.

DAY SEVEN

PSALM 31

For the choir director: A psalm of David.

¹O LORD, I have come to you for protection;
   don't let me be put to shame.
   Rescue me, for you always do what is right.
²Bend down and listen to me;
   rescue me quickly.
Be for me a great rock of safety,
   a fortress where my enemies cannot reach me.

³You are my rock and my fortress.
   For the honor of your name, lead me out of this peril.
⁴Pull me from the trap my enemies set for me,
   for I find protection in you alone.
⁵I entrust my spirit into your hand.
   Rescue me, LORD, for you are a faithful God.

⁶I hate those who worship worthless idols.
   I trust in the LORD.

[7]I am overcome with joy because of your unfailing love,
    for you have seen my troubles,
    and you care about the anguish of my soul.
[8]You have not handed me over to my enemy
    but have set me in a safe place.

[9]Have mercy on me, LORD, for I am in distress.
    My sight is blurred because of my tears.
    My body and soul are withering away.
[10]I am dying from grief;
    my years are shortened by sadness.
Misery has drained my strength;
    I am wasting away from within.
[11]I am scorned by all my enemies
    and despised by my neighbors—
    even my friends are afraid to come near me.
When they see me on the street,
    they turn the other way.
[12]I have been ignored as if I were dead,
    as if I were a broken pot.
[13]I have heard the many rumors about me,
    and I am surrounded by terror.
My enemies conspire against me,
    plotting to take my life.

¹⁴But I am trusting you, O LORD,
     saying, "You are my God!"
¹⁵My future is in your hands.
     Rescue me from those who hunt me down
          relentlessly.
¹⁶Let your favor shine on your servant.
     In your unfailing love, save me.
¹⁷Don't let me be disgraced, O LORD,
     for I call out to you for help.
Let the wicked be disgraced;
     let them lie silent in the grave.
¹⁸May their lying lips be silenced—
     those proud and arrogant lips that accuse the godly.

¹⁹Your goodness is so great!
     You have stored up great blessings for those who
          honor you.
You have done so much for those who come to you for
          protection,
     blessing them before the watching world.
²⁰You hide them in the shelter of your presence,
     safe from those who conspire against them.
You shelter them in your presence,
     far from accusing tongues.

²¹Praise the LORD,

> for he has shown me his unfailing love.
>
> He kept me safe when my city was under attack.

²²In sudden fear I had cried out,

> "I have been cut off from the LORD!"

But you heard my cry for mercy

> and answered my call for help.

²³Love the LORD, all you faithful ones!

> For the LORD protects those who are loyal to him,
>
> but he harshly punishes all who are arrogant.

²⁴So be strong and take courage,

> all you who put your hope in the LORD!

PSALM 32

A psalm of David.

¹Oh, what joy for those

> whose rebellion is forgiven,
>
> whose sin is put out of sight!

²Yes, what joy for those

> whose record the LORD has cleared of sin,
>
> whose lives are lived in complete honesty!

³When I refused to confess my sin,
　　I was weak and miserable,
　　and I groaned all day long.
⁴Day and night your hand of discipline was heavy on me.
　　My strength evaporated like water in the summer
　　　　heat.   *Interlude*

⁵Finally, I confessed all my sins to you
　　and stopped trying to hide them.
I said to myself, "I will confess my rebellion to the LORD."
　　And you forgave me! All my guilt is gone.   *Interlude*

⁶Therefore, let all the godly confess their rebellion to you
　　　　while there is time,
　　that they may not drown in the floodwaters of
　　　　judgment.
⁷For you are my hiding place;
　　you protect me from trouble.
　　You surround me with songs of victory.   *Interlude*

⁸The LORD says, "I will guide you along the best pathway
　　　　for your life.
　　I will advise you and watch over you.
⁹Do not be like a senseless horse or mule
　　that needs a bit and bridle to keep it under control."

¹⁰Many sorrows come to the wicked,
  but unfailing love surrounds those who trust the
    LORD.
¹¹So rejoice in the LORD and be glad, all you who obey him!
  Shout for joy, all you whose hearts are pure!

PSALM 33

¹Let the godly sing with joy to the LORD,
  for it is fitting to praise him.
²Praise the LORD with melodies on the lyre;
  make music for him on the ten-stringed harp.
³Sing new songs of praise to him;
  play skillfully on the harp and sing with joy.

⁴For the word of the LORD holds true,
  and everything he does is worthy of our trust.
⁵He loves whatever is just and good,
  and his unfailing love fills the earth.

⁶The LORD merely spoke,
  and the heavens were created.
He breathed the word,
  and all the stars were born.
⁷He gave the sea its boundaries
  and locked the oceans in vast reservoirs.

⁸Let everyone in the world fear the LORD,
    and let everyone stand in awe of him.
⁹For when he spoke, the world began!
    It appeared at his command.

¹⁰The LORD shatters the plans of the nations
    and thwarts all their schemes.
¹¹But the LORD's plans stand firm forever;
    his intentions can never be shaken.

¹²What joy for the nation whose God is the LORD,
    whose people he has chosen for his own.

¹³The LORD looks down from heaven
    and sees the whole human race.
¹⁴From his throne he observes
    all who live on the earth.
¹⁵He made their hearts,
    so he understands everything they do.
¹⁶The best-equipped army cannot save a king,
    nor is great strength enough to save a warrior.
¹⁷Don't count on your warhorse to give you victory—
    for all its strength, it cannot save you.

¹⁸But the LORD watches over those who fear him,
    those who rely on his unfailing love.

¹⁹He rescues them from death
   and keeps them alive in times of famine.

²⁰We depend on the LORD alone to save us.
   Only he can help us, protecting us like a shield.
²¹In him our hearts rejoice,
   for we are trusting in his holy name.
²²Let your unfailing love surround us, LORD,
   for our hope is in you alone.

PSALM 34

A psalm of David, regarding the time he pretended to be insane in front of Abimelech, who sent him away.

¹I will praise the LORD at all times.
   I will constantly speak his praises.
²I will boast only in the LORD;
   let all who are discouraged take heart.
³Come, let us tell of the LORD's greatness;
   let us exalt his name together.

⁴I prayed to the LORD, and he answered me,
   freeing me from all my fears.
⁵Those who look to him for help will be radiant with
      joy;
   no shadow of shame will darken their faces.

⁶I cried out to the LORD in my suffering, and he heard me.
  He set me free from all my fears.
⁷For the angel of the LORD guards all who fear him,
  and he rescues them.

⁸Taste and see that the LORD is good.
  Oh, the joys of those who trust in him!
⁹Let the LORD's people show him reverence,
  for those who honor him will have all they need.
¹⁰Even strong young lions sometimes go hungry,
  but those who trust in the LORD will never lack any
    good thing.

¹¹Come, my children, and listen to me,
  and I will teach you to fear the LORD.
¹²Do any of you want to live
  a life that is long and good?
¹³Then watch your tongue!
  Keep your lips from telling lies!
¹⁴Turn away from evil and do good.
  Work hard at living in peace with others.

¹⁵The eyes of the LORD watch over those who do right;
  his ears are open to their cries for help.
¹⁶But the LORD turns his face against those who do evil;
  he will erase their memory from the earth.

[17]The LORD hears his people when they call to him for
help.
He rescues them from all their troubles.
[18]The LORD is close to the brokenhearted;
he rescues those who are crushed in spirit.

[19]The righteous face many troubles,
but the LORD rescues them from each and every one.
[20]For the LORD protects them from harm—
not one of their bones will be broken!

[21]Calamity will surely overtake the wicked,
and those who hate the righteous will be punished.
[22]But the LORD will redeem those who serve him.
Everyone who trusts in him will be freely pardoned.

PSALM 35

A psalm of David.

[1]O LORD, oppose those who oppose me.
Declare war on those who are attacking me.
[2]Put on your armor, and take up your shield.
Prepare for battle, and come to my aid.
[3]Lift up your spear and javelin
and block the way of my enemies.

Let me hear you say,
    "I am your salvation!"

⁴Humiliate and disgrace those trying to kill me;
    turn them back in confusion.
⁵Blow them away like chaff in the wind—
    a wind sent by the angel of the LORD.
⁶Make their path dark and slippery,
    with the angel of the LORD pursuing them.
⁷Although I did them no wrong,
    they laid a trap for me.
Although I did them no wrong,
    they dug a pit for me.
⁸So let sudden ruin overtake them!
    Let them be caught in the snare they set for me!
    Let them fall to destruction in the pit they dug
        for me.

⁹Then I will rejoice in the LORD.
    I will be glad because he rescues me.
¹⁰I will praise him from the bottom of my heart:
    "LORD, who can compare with you?
Who else rescues the weak and helpless from the strong?
    Who else protects the poor and needy from those
        who want to rob them?"

¹¹Malicious witnesses testify against me.
  They accuse me of things I don't even know about.
¹²They repay me with evil for the good I do.
  I am sick with despair.
¹³Yet when they were ill,
  I grieved for them.
I even fasted and prayed for them,
  but my prayers returned unanswered.
¹⁴I was sad, as though they were my friends or family,
  as if I were grieving for my own mother.

¹⁵But they are glad now that I am in trouble;
  they gleefully join together against me.
I am attacked by people I don't even know;
  they hurl slander at me continually.
¹⁶They mock me with the worst kind of profanity,
  and they snarl at me.

¹⁷How long, O Lord, will you look on and do nothing?
  Rescue me from their fierce attacks.
  Protect my life from these lions!
¹⁸Then I will thank you in front of the entire congregation.
  I will praise you before all the people.

¹⁹Don't let my treacherous enemies
  rejoice over my defeat.

Don't let those who hate me without cause
    gloat over my sorrow.
²⁰They don't talk of peace;
    they plot against innocent people
    who are minding their own business.
²¹They shout that they have seen me doing wrong.
    "Aha," they say. "Aha!
    With our own eyes we saw him do it!"

²²O LORD, you know all about this.
    Do not stay silent.
    Don't abandon me now, O Lord.
²³Wake up! Rise to my defense!
    Take up my case, my God and my Lord.
²⁴Declare me "not guilty," O LORD my God, for you give
        justice.
    Don't let my enemies laugh about me in my
        troubles.
²⁵Don't let them say, "Look! We have what we wanted!
    Now we will eat him alive!"

²⁶May those who rejoice at my troubles
    be humiliated and disgraced.
May those who triumph over me
    be covered with shame and dishonor.

²⁷But give great joy to those
who have stood with me in my defense.
Let them continually say, "Great is the LORD,
who enjoys helping his servant."
²⁸Then I will tell everyone of your justice and goodness,
and I will praise you all day long.

PROVERBS 7

Follow my advice, my son; always treasure my commands.
²Obey them and live! Guard my teachings as your most precious possession. ³Tie them on your fingers as a reminder. Write them deep within your heart.

⁴Love wisdom like a sister; make insight a beloved member of your family. ⁵Let them hold you back from an affair with an immoral woman, from listening to the flattery of an adulterous woman.

⁶I was looking out the window of my house one day ⁷and saw a simpleminded young man who lacked common sense. ⁸He was crossing the street near the house of an immoral woman. He was strolling down the path by her house ⁹at twilight, as the day was fading, as the dark of night set in. ¹⁰The woman approached him, dressed seductively and sly of heart. ¹¹She was the brash, rebellious type

who never stays at home. ¹²She is often seen in the streets and markets, soliciting at every corner.

¹³She threw her arms around him and kissed him, and with a brazen look she said, ¹⁴"I've offered my sacrifices and just finished my vows. ¹⁵It's you I was looking for! I came out to find you, and here you are! ¹⁶My bed is spread with colored sheets of finest linen imported from Egypt. ¹⁷I've perfumed my bed with myrrh, aloes, and cinnamon. ¹⁸Come, let's drink our fill of love until morning. Let's enjoy each other's caresses, ¹⁹for my husband is not home. He's away on a long trip. ²⁰He has taken a wallet full of money with him, and he won't return until later in the month."

²¹So she seduced him with her pretty speech. With her flattery she enticed him. ²²He followed her at once, like an ox going to the slaughter or like a trapped stag, ²³awaiting the arrow that would pierce its heart. He was like a bird flying into a snare, little knowing it would cost him his life.

²⁴Listen to me, my sons, and pay attention to my words. ²⁵Don't let your hearts stray away toward her. Don't wander down her wayward path. ²⁶For she has been the ruin of many; numerous men have been her victims. ²⁷Her house is the road to the grave. Her bedroom is the den of death.

DAY EIGHT

PSALM 36

For the choir director: A psalm of David, the servant of the LORD.

¹Sin whispers to the wicked, deep within their hearts.
    They have no fear of God to restrain them.
²In their blind conceit,
    they cannot see how wicked they really are.
³Everything they say is crooked and deceitful.
    They refuse to act wisely or do what is good.
⁴They lie awake at night, hatching sinful plots.
    Their course of action is never good.
    They make no attempt to turn from evil.

⁵Your unfailing love, O LORD, is as vast as the
        heavens;
    your faithfulness reaches beyond the clouds.
⁶Your righteousness is like the mighty mountains,
    your justice like the ocean depths.
You care for people and animals alike, O LORD.
⁷   How precious is your unfailing love, O God!

All humanity finds shelter
> in the shadow of your wings.
8You feed them from the abundance of your own house,
> letting them drink from your rivers of delight.
9For you are the fountain of life,
> the light by which we see.

10Pour out your unfailing love on those who love you;
> give justice to those with honest hearts.
11Don't let the proud trample me;
> don't let the wicked push me around.
12Look! They have fallen!
> They have been thrown down, never to rise again.

PSALM 37

A psalm of David.

1Don't worry about the wicked.
> Don't envy those who do wrong.
2For like grass, they soon fade away.
> Like springtime flowers, they soon wither.

3Trust in the LORD and do good.
> Then you will live safely in the land and prosper.
4Take delight in the LORD,
> and he will give you your heart's desires.

⁵Commit everything you do to the Lord.
　　Trust him, and he will help you.
⁶He will make your innocence as clear as the dawn,
　　and the justice of your cause will shine like the
　　　　noonday sun.

⁷Be still in the presence of the Lord,
　　and wait patiently for him to act.
Don't worry about evil people who prosper
　　or fret about their wicked schemes.

⁸Stop your anger!
　　Turn from your rage!
Do not envy others—
　　it only leads to harm.
⁹For the wicked will be destroyed,
　　but those who trust in the Lord will possess the land.

¹⁰In a little while, the wicked will disappear.
　　Though you look for them, they will be gone.
¹¹Those who are gentle and lowly will possess the land;
　　they will live in prosperous security.

¹²The wicked plot against the godly;
　　they snarl at them in defiance.
¹³But the Lord just laughs,
　　for he sees their day of judgment coming.

¹⁴The wicked draw their swords
    and string their bows
to kill the poor and the oppressed,
    to slaughter those who do right.
¹⁵But they will be stabbed through the heart with their
        own swords,
    and their bows will be broken.

¹⁶It is better to be godly and have little
    than to be evil and possess much.
¹⁷For the strength of the wicked will be shattered,
    but the LORD takes care of the godly.

¹⁸Day by day the LORD takes care of the innocent,
    and they will receive a reward that lasts forever.
¹⁹They will survive through hard times;
    even in famine they will have more than enough.

²⁰But the wicked will perish.
    The LORD's enemies are like flowers in a field—
    they will disappear like smoke.

²¹The wicked borrow and never repay,
    but the godly are generous givers.
²²Those blessed by the LORD will inherit the land,
    but those cursed by him will die.

²³The steps of the godly are directed by the LORD.
  He delights in every detail of their lives.
²⁴Though they stumble, they will not fall,
  for the LORD holds them by the hand.

²⁵Once I was young, and now I am old.
  Yet I have never seen the godly forsaken,
  nor seen their children begging for bread.
²⁶The godly always give generous loans to others,
  and their children are a blessing.

²⁷Turn from evil and do good,
  and you will live in the land forever.
²⁸For the LORD loves justice,
  and he will never abandon the godly.

He will keep them safe forever,
  but the children of the wicked will perish.
²⁹The godly will inherit the land
  and will live there forever.

³⁰The godly offer good counsel;
  they know what is right from wrong.
³¹They fill their hearts with God's law,
  so they will never slip from his path.

³²Those who are evil spy on the godly,
  waiting for an excuse to kill them.
³³But the LORD will not let the wicked succeed
  or let the godly be condemned when they are brought
    before the judge.

³⁴Don't be impatient for the LORD to act!
  Travel steadily along his path.
He will honor you, giving you the land.
  You will see the wicked destroyed.

³⁵I myself have seen it happen—
  proud and evil people thriving like mighty trees.
³⁶But when I looked again, they were gone!
  Though I searched for them, I could not find them!

³⁷Look at those who are honest and good,
  for a wonderful future lies before those who love peace.
³⁸But the wicked will be destroyed;
  they have no future.

³⁹The LORD saves the godly;
  he is their fortress in times of trouble.
⁴⁰The LORD helps them,
  rescuing them from the wicked.
He saves them,
  and they find shelter in him.

PSALM 38

A psalm of David, to bring us to the LORD's remembrance.

¹O LORD, don't rebuke me in your anger!
　　Don't discipline me in your rage!
²Your arrows have struck deep,
　　and your blows are crushing me.

³Because of your anger, my whole body is sick;
　　my health is broken because of my sins.
⁴My guilt overwhelms me—
　　it is a burden too heavy to bear.
⁵My wounds fester and stink
　　because of my foolish sins.
⁶I am bent over and racked with pain.
　　My days are filled with grief.
⁷A raging fever burns within me,
　　and my health is broken.
⁸I am exhausted and completely crushed.
　　My groans come from an anguished heart.

⁹You know what I long for, Lord;
　　you hear my every sigh.
¹⁰My heart beats wildly, my strength fails,
　　and I am going blind.

¹¹My loved ones and friends stay away, fearing my
　　disease.
　　Even my own family stands at a distance.
¹²Meanwhile, my enemies lay traps for me;
　　they make plans to ruin me.
　　They think up treacherous deeds all day long.
¹³But I am deaf to all their threats.
　　I am silent before them as one who cannot speak.
¹⁴I choose to hear nothing,
　　and I make no reply.

¹⁵For I am waiting for you, O LORD.
　　You must answer for me, O Lord my God.
¹⁶I prayed, "Don't let my enemies gloat over me
　　or rejoice at my downfall."
¹⁷I am on the verge of collapse,
　　facing constant pain.
¹⁸But I confess my sins;
　　I am deeply sorry for what I have done.
¹⁹My enemies are many;
　　they hate me though I have done nothing against
　　　them.
²⁰They repay me evil for good
　　and oppose me because I stand for the right.

²¹Do not abandon me, LORD.

Do not stand at a distance, my God.
²²Come quickly to help me, O Lord my savior.

PSALM 39

For Jeduthun, the choir director: A psalm of David.

¹I said to myself, "I will watch what I do
and not sin in what I say.
I will curb my tongue
when the ungodly are around me."
²But as I stood there in silence—
not even speaking of good things—
the turmoil within me grew to the bursting point.
³My thoughts grew hot within me
and began to burn,
igniting a fire of words:
⁴"LORD, remind me how brief my time on earth will be.
Remind me that my days are numbered,
and that my life is fleeing away.
⁵My life is no longer than the width of my hand.
An entire lifetime is just a moment to you;
human existence is but a breath."   *Interlude*

⁶We are merely moving shadows,
    and all our busy rushing ends in nothing.
    We heap up wealth for someone else to spend.

⁷And so, Lord, where do I put my hope?
    My only hope is in you.
⁸Rescue me from my rebellion,
    for even fools mock me when I rebel.
⁹I am silent before you; I won't say a word.
    For my punishment is from you.
¹⁰Please, don't punish me anymore!
    I am exhausted by the blows from your hand.
¹¹When you discipline people for their sins,
    their lives can be crushed like the life of a moth.
    Human existence is as frail as breath.   *Interlude*

¹²Hear my prayer, O LORD!
    Listen to my cries for help!
    Don't ignore my tears.
For I am your guest—
    a traveler passing through,
    as my ancestors were before me.
¹³Spare me so I can smile again
    before I am gone and exist no more.

For the choir director: A psalm of David.

¹I waited patiently for the LORD to help me,
    and he turned to me and heard my cry.
²He lifted me out of the pit of despair,
    out of the mud and the mire.
He set my feet on solid ground
    and steadied me as I walked along.
³He has given me a new song to sing,
    a hymn of praise to our God.
Many will see what he has done and be astounded.
    They will put their trust in the LORD.

⁴Oh, the joys of those who trust the LORD,
    who have no confidence in the proud,
    or in those who worship idols.
⁵O LORD my God, you have done many miracles for us.
    Your plans for us are too numerous to list.
If I tried to recite all your wonderful deeds,
    I would never come to the end of them.

⁶You take no delight in sacrifices or offerings.
    Now that you have made me listen, I finally understand—
    you don't require burnt offerings or sin offerings.

⁷Then I said, "Look, I have come.

And this has been written about me in your scroll:
⁸I take joy in doing your will, my God,

for your law is written on my heart."

⁹I have told all your people about your justice.

I have not been afraid to speak out,

as you, O LORD, well know.
¹⁰I have not kept this good news hidden in my heart;

I have talked about your faithfulness and saving

power.

I have told everyone in the great assembly

of your unfailing love and faithfulness.

¹¹LORD, don't hold back your tender mercies from me.

My only hope is in your unfailing love and

faithfulness.
¹²For troubles surround me—

too many to count!

They pile up so high

I can't see my way out.

They are more numerous than the hairs on my head.

I have lost all my courage.

¹³Please, LORD, rescue me!

Come quickly, LORD, and help me.

¹⁴May those who try to destroy me
    be humiliated and put to shame.
May those who take delight in my trouble
    be turned back in disgrace.
¹⁵Let them be horrified by their shame,
    for they said, "Aha! We've got him now!"

¹⁶But may all who search for you
    be filled with joy and gladness.
May those who love your salvation
    repeatedly shout, "The LORD is great!"

¹⁷As for me, I am poor and needy,
    but the Lord is thinking about me right now.
You are my helper and my savior.
    Do not delay, O my God.

PROVERBS 8

Listen as wisdom calls out! Hear as understanding raises her voice! ²She stands on the hilltop and at the crossroads. ³At the entrance to the city, at the city gates, she cries aloud, ⁴"I call to you, to all of you! I am raising my voice to all people. ⁵How naive you are! Let me give you common sense. O foolish ones, let me give you under-standing. ⁶Listen to me! For I have excellent things to tell you. Everything I say is right, [7]for I speak the truth and hate every kind of deception. [8]My advice is wholesome and good. There is nothing crooked or twisted in it. [9]My words are plain to anyone with understanding, clear to those who want to learn.

[10]"Choose my instruction rather than silver, and knowledge over pure gold. [11]For wisdom is far more valuable than rubies. Nothing you desire can be compared with it.

[12]"I, Wisdom, live together with good judgment. I know where to discover knowledge and discernment. [13]All who fear the LORD will hate evil. That is why I hate pride, arrogance, corruption, and perverted speech. [14]Good advice and success belong to me. Insight and strength are mine. [15]Because of me, kings reign, and rulers make just laws. [16]Rulers lead with my help, and nobles make righteous judgments.

[17]"I love all who love me. Those who search for me will surely find me. [18]Unending riches, honor, wealth, and justice are mine to distribute. [19]My gifts are better than the purest gold, my wages better than sterling silver! [20]I walk in righteousness, in paths of justice. [21]Those who love me inherit wealth, for I fill their treasuries.

[22]"The LORD formed me from the beginning, before he created anything else. [23]I was appointed in ages past, at

the very first, before the earth began. ²⁴I was born before the oceans were created, before the springs bubbled forth their waters. ²⁵Before the mountains and the hills were formed, I was born—²⁶before he had made the earth and fields and the first handfuls of soil.

²⁷"I was there when he established the heavens, when he drew the horizon on the oceans. ²⁸I was there when he set the clouds above, when he established the deep fountains of the earth. ²⁹I was there when he set the limits of the seas, so they would not spread beyond their boundaries. And when he marked off the earth's foundations, ³⁰I was the architect at his side. I was his constant delight, rejoicing always in his presence. ³¹And how happy I was with what he created—his wide world and all the human family!

³²"And so, my children, listen to me, for happy are all who follow my ways. ³³Listen to my counsel and be wise. Don't ignore it.

³⁴"Happy are those who listen to me, watching for me daily at my gates, waiting for me outside my home! ³⁵For whoever finds me finds life and wins approval from the LORD. ³⁶But those who miss me have injured themselves. All who hate me love death."

DAY NINE

PSALM 41

For the choir director: A psalm of David.

¹Oh, the joys of those who are kind to the poor.
　　The LORD rescues them in times of trouble.
²The LORD protects them
　　and keeps them alive.
He gives them prosperity
　　and rescues them from their enemies.
³The LORD nurses them when they are sick
　　and eases their pain and discomfort.

⁴"O LORD," I prayed, "have mercy on me.
　　Heal me, for I have sinned against you."
⁵But my enemies say nothing but evil about me.
　　"How soon will he die and be forgotten?" they ask.
⁶They visit me as if they are my friends,
　　but all the while they gather gossip,
　　and when they leave, they spread it everywhere.

⁷All who hate me whisper about me,
  imagining the worst for me.
⁸"Whatever he has, it is fatal," they say.
  "He will never get out of that bed!"
⁹Even my best friend, the one I trusted completely,
  the one who shared my food,
  has turned against me.

¹⁰LORD, have mercy on me.
  Make me well again, so I can pay them back!
¹¹I know that you are pleased with me,
  for you have not let my enemy triumph over me.
¹²You have preserved my life because I am innocent;
  you have brought me into your presence forever.

¹³Bless the LORD, the God of Israel,
  who lives forever from eternal ages past.
  Amen and amen!

BOOK TWO (Psalms 42–72)

PSALM 42

For the choir director: A psalm of the descendants of Korah.

¹As the deer pants for streams of water,
  so I long for you, O God.

²I thirst for God, the living God.
  When can I come and stand before him?
³Day and night, I have only tears for food,
  while my enemies continually taunt me, saying,
  "Where is this God of yours?"

⁴My heart is breaking
  as I remember how it used to be:
I walked among the crowds of worshipers,
  leading a great procession to the house of God,
singing for joy and giving thanks—
  it was the sound of a great celebration!

⁵Why am I discouraged?
  Why so sad?
I will put my hope in God!
  I will praise him again—
  my Savior and ⁶my God!

Now I am deeply discouraged,
  but I will remember your kindness—
from Mount Hermon, the source of the Jordan,
  from the land of Mount Mizar.
⁷I hear the tumult of the raging seas
  as your waves and surging tides sweep over me.

⁸Through each day the LORD pours his unfailing love upon me,
  and through each night I sing his songs,
    praying to God who gives me life.

⁹"O God my rock," I cry,
    "Why have you forsaken me?
Why must I wander in darkness,
    oppressed by my enemies?"
¹⁰Their taunts pierce me like a fatal wound.
    They scoff, "Where is this God of yours?"

¹¹Why am I discouraged?
    Why so sad?
I will put my hope in God!
    I will praise him again—
      my Savior and my God!

PSALM 43

¹O God, take up my cause!
    Defend me against these ungodly people.
    Rescue me from these unjust liars.
²For you are God, my only safe haven.
    Why have you tossed me aside?
Why must I wander around in darkness,
    oppressed by my enemies?

³Send out your light and your truth;
 let them guide me.
Let them lead me to your holy mountain,
 to the place where you live.
⁴There I will go to the altar of God,
 to God—the source of all my joy.
I will praise you with my harp,
 O God, my God!

⁵Why am I discouraged?
 Why so sad?
I will put my hope in God!
 I will praise him again—
 my Savior and my God!

PSALM 44

For the choir director: A psalm of the descendants of Korah.

¹O God, we have heard it with our own ears—
 our ancestors have told us
of all you did in other days,
 in days long ago:
²You drove out the pagan nations
 and gave all the land to our ancestors;

you crushed their enemies,
    setting our ancestors free.
³They did not conquer the land with their swords;
    it was not their own strength that gave them victory.
It was by your mighty power that they succeeded;
    it was because you favored them and smiled on them.

⁴You are my King and my God.
    You command victories for your people.
⁵Only by your power can we push back our enemies;
    only in your name can we trample our foes.
⁶I do not trust my bow;
    I do not count on my sword to save me.
⁷It is you who gives us victory over our enemies;
    it is you who humbles those who hate us.
⁸O God, we give glory to you all day long
    and constantly praise your name.   *Interlude*

⁹But now you have tossed us aside in dishonor.
    You no longer lead our armies to battle.
¹⁰You make us retreat from our enemies
    and allow them to plunder our land.
¹¹You have treated us like sheep waiting to be
        slaughtered;
    you have scattered us among the nations.

¹²You sold us—your precious people—for a pittance.
　　You valued us at nothing at all.

¹³You have caused all our neighbors to mock us.
　　We are an object of scorn and derision to the nations
　　　around us.
¹⁴You have made us the butt of their jokes;
　　we are scorned by the whole world.
¹⁵We can't escape the constant humiliation;
　　shame is written across our faces.
¹⁶All we hear are the taunts of our mockers.
　　All we see are our vengeful enemies.

¹⁷All this has happened despite our loyalty to you.
　　We have not violated your covenant.
¹⁸Our hearts have not deserted you.
　　We have not strayed from your path.
¹⁹Yet you have crushed us in the desert.
　　You have covered us with darkness and death.

²⁰If we had turned away from worshiping our God
　　or spread our hands in prayer to foreign gods,
²¹God would surely have known it,
　　for he knows the secrets of every heart.
²²For your sake we are killed every day;
　　we are being slaughtered like sheep.

²³Wake up, O Lord! Why do you sleep?
   Get up! Do not reject us forever.
²⁴Why do you look the other way?
   Why do you ignore our suffering and oppression?
²⁵We collapse in the dust,
   lying face down in the dirt.
²⁶Rise up! Come and help us!
   Save us because of your unfailing love.

PSALM 45

For the choir director: A psalm of the descendants of Korah, to be sung to the tune "Lilies." A love song.

¹My heart overflows with a beautiful thought!
   I will recite a lovely poem to the king,
      for my tongue is like the pen of a skillful poet.

²You are the most handsome of all.
   Gracious words stream from your lips.
   God himself has blessed you forever.
³Put on your sword, O mighty warrior!
   You are so glorious, so majestic!
⁴In your majesty, ride out to victory,
   defending truth, humility, and justice.
   Go forth to perform awe-inspiring deeds!

⁵Your arrows are sharp,
    piercing your enemies' hearts.
The nations fall before you,
    lying down beneath your feet.

⁶Your throne, O God, endures forever and ever.
    Your royal power is expressed in justice.
⁷You love what is right and hate what is wrong.
    Therefore God, your God, has anointed you,
    pouring out the oil of joy on you more than on
        anyone else.
⁸Your robes are perfumed with myrrh, aloes, and cassia.
    In palaces decorated with ivory,
    you are entertained by the music of harps.
⁹Kings' daughters are among your concubines.
    At your right side stands the queen,
    wearing jewelry of finest gold from Ophir!

¹⁰Listen to me, O royal daughter; take to heart what
        I say.
    Forget your people and your homeland far away.
¹¹For your royal husband delights in your beauty;
    honor him, for he is your lord.
¹²The princes of Tyre will shower you with gifts.
    People of great wealth will entreat your favor.

¹³The bride, a princess, waits within her chamber,
> dressed in a gown woven with gold.
¹⁴In her beautiful robes, she is led to the king,
> accompanied by her bridesmaids.
¹⁵What a joyful, enthusiastic procession
> as they enter the king's palace!

¹⁶Your sons will become kings like their father.
> You will make them rulers over many lands.

¹⁷I will bring honor to your name in every generation.
> Therefore, the nations will praise you forever and
> ever.

PROVERBS 9

Wisdom has built her spacious house with seven pillars.
²She has prepared a great banquet, mixed the wines, and
set the table. ³She has sent her servants to invite everyone
to come. She calls out from the heights overlooking the
city. ⁴"Come home with me," she urges the simple. To
those without good judgment, she says, ⁵"Come, eat my
food, and drink the wine I have mixed. ⁶Leave your foolish
ways behind, and begin to live; learn how to be wise."

> ⁷Anyone who rebukes a mocker will get a smart
retort. Anyone who rebukes the wicked will get hurt. ⁸So

don't bother rebuking mockers; they will only hate you. But the wise, when rebuked, will love you all the more. ⁹Teach the wise, and they will be wiser. Teach the righteous, and they will learn more.

¹⁰Fear of the LORD is the beginning of wisdom. Knowledge of the Holy One results in understanding.

¹¹Wisdom will multiply your days and add years to your life. ¹²If you become wise, you will be the one to benefit. If you scorn wisdom, you will be the one to suffer.

¹³The woman named Folly is loud and brash. She is ignorant and doesn't even know it. ¹⁴She sits in her doorway on the heights overlooking the city. ¹⁵She calls out to men going by who are minding their own business. ¹⁶ "Come home with me," she urges the simple. To those without good judgment, she says, ¹⁷"Stolen water is refreshing; food eaten in secret tastes the best!" ¹⁸But the men don't realize that her former guests are now in the grave.

DAY TEN

PSALM 46

For the choir director: A psalm of the descendants of Korah, to be sung by soprano voices. A song.

¹God is our refuge and strength,
   always ready to help in times of trouble.
²So we will not fear, even if earthquakes come
   and the mountains crumble into the sea.
³Let the oceans roar and foam.
   Let the mountains tremble as the waters surge!

Interlude

⁴A river brings joy to the city of our God,
   the sacred home of the Most High.
⁵God himself lives in that city; it cannot be destroyed.
   God will protect it at the break of day.
⁶The nations are in an uproar,
   and kingdoms crumble!
God thunders,
   and the earth melts!

⁷The LORD Almighty is here among us;
    the God of Israel is our fortress.   *Interlude*

⁸Come, see the glorious works of the LORD:
    See how he brings destruction upon the world
⁹and causes wars to end throughout the earth.
    He breaks the bow and snaps the spear in two;
    he burns the shields with fire.

¹⁰"Be silent, and know that I am God!
    I will be honored by every nation.
    I will be honored throughout the world."

¹¹The LORD Almighty is here among us;
    the God of Israel is our fortress.   *Interlude*

PSALM 47

For the choir director: A psalm of the descendants of Korah.

¹Come, everyone, and clap your hands for joy!
    Shout to God with joyful praise!
²For the LORD Most High is awesome.
    He is the great King of all the earth.
³He subdues the nations before us,
    putting our enemies beneath our feet.

⁴He chose the Promised Land as our inheritance,
  the proud possession of Jacob's descendants, whom
    he loves.   *Interlude*

⁵God has ascended with a mighty shout.
  The LORD has ascended with trumpets blaring.
⁶Sing praise to God, sing praises;
  sing praise to our King, sing praises!

⁷For God is the King over all the earth.
  Praise him with a psalm!
⁸God reigns above the nations,
  sitting on his holy throne.
⁹The rulers of the world have gathered together.
  They join us in praising the God of Abraham.
For all the kings of the earth belong to God.
  He is highly honored everywhere.

PSALM 48

A psalm of the descendants of Korah. A song.

¹How great is the LORD,
  and how much we should praise him
in the city of our God,
  which is on his holy mountain!

²It is magnificent in elevation—
 the whole earth rejoices to see it!
Mount Zion, the holy mountain,
 is the city of the great King!
³God himself is in Jerusalem's towers.
 He reveals himself as her defender.

⁴The kings of the earth joined forces
 and advanced against the city.
⁵But when they saw it, they were stunned;
 they were terrified and ran away.
⁶They were gripped with terror,
 like a woman writhing in the pain of childbirth
⁷or like the mighty ships of Tarshish
 being shattered by a powerful east wind.

⁸We had heard of the city's glory,
 but now we have seen it ourselves—
 the city of the LORD Almighty.
It is the city of our God;
 he will make it safe forever. *Interlude*

⁹O God, we meditate on your unfailing love
 as we worship in your Temple.
¹⁰As your name deserves, O God,
 you will be praised to the ends of the earth.

Your strong right hand is filled with victory.

¹¹Let the people on Mount Zion rejoice.

Let the towns of Judah be glad,

for your judgments are just.

¹²Go, inspect the city of Jerusalem.

Walk around and count the many towers.

¹³Take note of the fortified walls,

and tour all the citadels,

that you may describe them

to future generations.

¹⁴For that is what God is like.

He is our God forever and ever,

and he will be our guide until we die.

PSALM 49

For the choir director: A psalm of the descendants of Korah.

¹Listen to this, all you people!

Pay attention, everyone in the world!

²High and low,

rich and poor—listen!

³For my words are wise,

and my thoughts are filled with insight.

[4]I listen carefully to many proverbs
and solve riddles with inspiration from a harp.

[5]There is no need to fear when times of trouble come,
when enemies are surrounding me.
[6]They trust in their wealth
and boast of great riches.
[7]Yet they cannot redeem themselves from death
by paying a ransom to God.
[8]Redemption does not come so easily,
for no one can ever pay enough
[9]to live forever
and never see the grave.

[10]Those who are wise must finally die,
just like the foolish and senseless,
leaving all their wealth behind.
[11]The grave is their eternal home,
where they will stay forever.
They may name their estates after themselves,
but they leave their wealth to others.
[12]They will not last long despite their riches—
they will die like the animals.
[13]This is the fate of fools,
though they will be remembered as being so wise.

Interlude

¹⁴Like sheep, they are led to the grave,
  where death will be their shepherd.
In the morning the godly will rule over them.
  Their bodies will rot in the grave,
  far from their grand estates.
¹⁵But as for me, God will redeem my life.
  He will snatch me from the power of death.   *Interlude*

¹⁶So don't be dismayed when the wicked grow rich,
  and their homes become ever more splendid.
¹⁷For when they die, they carry nothing with them.
  Their wealth will not follow them into the grave.
¹⁸In this life they consider themselves fortunate,
  and the world loudly applauds their success.
¹⁹But they will die like all others before them
  and never again see the light of day.
²⁰People who boast of their wealth don't understand
  that they will die like the animals.

PSALM 50

A psalm of Asaph.

¹The mighty God, the LORD, has spoken;
  he has summoned all humanity from east to west!

²From Mount Zion, the perfection of beauty,
  God shines in glorious radiance.
³Our God approaches with the noise of thunder.
  Fire devours everything in his way,
  and a great storm rages around him.
⁴Heaven and earth will be his witnesses
  as he judges his people:
⁵"Bring my faithful people to me—
  those who made a covenant with me by giving
    sacrifices."
⁶Then let the heavens proclaim his justice,
  for God himself will be the judge.   *Interlude*

⁷"O my people, listen as I speak.
  Here are my charges against you, O Israel:
  I am God, your God!
⁸I have no complaint about your sacrifices
  or the burnt offerings you constantly bring to my
    altar.
⁹But I want no more bulls from your barns;
  I want no more goats from your pens.
¹⁰For all the animals of the forest are mine,
  and I own the cattle on a thousand hills.
¹¹Every bird of the mountains
  and all the animals of the field belong to me.

¹²If I were hungry, I would not mention it to you,
    for all the world is mine and everything in it.
¹³I don't need the bulls you sacrifice;
    I don't need the blood of goats.
¹⁴What I want instead is your true thanks to God;
    I want you to fulfill your vows to the Most High.
¹⁵Trust me in your times of trouble,
    and I will rescue you,
    and you will give me glory."

¹⁶But God says to the wicked:
    "Recite my laws no longer,
    and don't pretend that you obey me.
¹⁷For you refuse my discipline
    and treat my laws like trash.
¹⁸When you see a thief, you help him,
    and you spend your time with adulterers.
¹⁹Your mouths are filled with wickedness,
    and your tongues are full of lies.
²⁰You sit around and slander a brother—
    your own mother's son.
²¹While you did all this, I remained silent,
    and you thought I didn't care.
But now I will rebuke you,
    listing all my charges against you.

²²Repent, all of you who ignore me,

    or I will tear you apart,

    and no one will help you.

²³But giving thanks is a sacrifice that truly honors me.

    If you keep to my path,

    I will reveal to you the salvation of God."

PROVERBS 10

The proverbs of Solomon:

A wise child brings joy to a father; a foolish child brings grief to a mother.

²Ill-gotten gain has no lasting value, but right living can save your life.

³The LORD will not let the godly starve to death, but he refuses to satisfy the craving of the wicked.

⁴Lazy people are soon poor; hard workers get rich.

⁵A wise youth works hard all summer; a youth who sleeps away the hour of opportunity brings shame.

⁶The godly are showered with blessings; evil people cover up their harmful intentions.

⁷We all have happy memories of the godly, but the name of a wicked person rots away.

⁸The wise are glad to be instructed, but babbling fools fall flat on their faces.

⁹People with integrity have firm footing, but those who follow crooked paths will slip and fall.

¹⁰People who wink at wrong cause trouble, but a bold reproof promotes peace.

¹¹The words of the godly lead to life; evil people cover up their harmful intentions.

¹²Hatred stirs up quarrels, but love covers all offenses.

¹³Wise words come from the lips of people with understanding, but fools will be punished with a rod.

¹⁴Wise people treasure knowledge, but the babbling of a fool invites trouble.

¹⁵The wealth of the rich is their fortress; the poverty of the poor is their calamity.

¹⁶The earnings of the godly enhance their lives, but evil people squander their money on sin.

¹⁷People who accept correction are on the pathway to life, but those who ignore it will lead others astray.

¹⁸To hide hatred is to be a liar; to slander is to be a fool.

¹⁹Don't talk too much, for it fosters sin. Be sensible and turn off the flow!

²⁰The words of the godly are like sterling silver; the heart of a fool is worthless.

²¹The godly give good advice, but fools are destroyed by their lack of common sense.

²²The blessing of the LORD makes a person rich, and he adds no sorrow with it.

²³Doing wrong is fun for a fool, while wise conduct is a pleasure to the wise.

²⁴The fears of the wicked will all come true; so will the hopes of the godly.

²⁵Disaster strikes like a cyclone, whirling the wicked away, but the godly have a lasting foundation.

²⁶Lazy people are a pain to their employer. They are like smoke in the eyes or vinegar that sets the teeth on edge.

²⁷Fear of the LORD lengthens one's life, but the years of the wicked are cut short.

²⁸The hopes of the godly result in happiness, but the expectations of the wicked are all in vain.

²⁹The LORD protects the upright but destroys the wicked.

³⁰The godly will never be disturbed, but the wicked will be removed from the land.

³¹The godly person gives wise advice, but the tongue that deceives will be cut off.

³²The godly speak words that are helpful, but the wicked speak only what is corrupt.

DAY ELEVEN

PSALM 51

For the choir director: A psalm of David, regarding the time Nathan the prophet came to him after David had committed adultery with Bathsheba.

¹Have mercy on me, O God,
  because of your unfailing love.
Because of your great compassion,
  blot out the stain of my sins.
²Wash me clean from my guilt.
  Purify me from my sin.

³For I recognize my shameful deeds—
  they haunt me day and night.
⁴Against you, and you alone, have I sinned;
  I have done what is evil in your sight.
You will be proved right in what you say,
  and your judgment against me is just.

⁵For I was born a sinner—
  yes, from the moment my mother conceived me.

⁶But you desire honesty from the heart,
  so you can teach me to be wise in my inmost being.

⁷Purify me from my sins, and I will be clean;
  wash me, and I will be whiter than snow.
⁸Oh, give me back my joy again;
  you have broken me—
  now let me rejoice.
⁹Don't keep looking at my sins.
  Remove the stain of my guilt.
¹⁰Create in me a clean heart, O God.
  Renew a right spirit within me.
¹¹Do not banish me from your presence,
  and don't take your Holy Spirit from me.
¹²Restore to me again the joy of your salvation,
  and make me willing to obey you.
¹³Then I will teach your ways to sinners,
  and they will return to you.
¹⁴Forgive me for shedding blood, O God who saves;
  then I will joyfully sing of your forgiveness.
¹⁵Unseal my lips, O Lord,
  that I may praise you.

¹⁶You would not be pleased with sacrifices,
  or I would bring them.

If I brought you a burnt offering,
>you would not accept it.
¹⁷The sacrifice you want is a broken spirit.
>A broken and repentant heart, O God,
>you will not despise.

¹⁸Look with favor on Zion and help her;
>rebuild the walls of Jerusalem.
¹⁹Then you will be pleased with worthy sacrifices
>and with our whole burnt offerings;
>and bulls will again be sacrificed on your altar.

PSALM 52

For the choir director: A psalm of David, regarding the time Doeg the Edomite told Saul that Ahimelech had given refuge to David.

¹You call yourself a hero, do you?
>Why boast about this crime of yours,
>you who have disgraced God's people?
²All day long you plot destruction.
>Your tongue cuts like a sharp razor;
>you're an expert at telling lies.
³You love evil more than good
>and lies more than truth.   *Interlude*

⁴You love to say things that harm others,
    you liar!
⁵But God will strike you down once and for all.
    He will pull you from your home
    and drag you from the land of the living.   *Interlude*

⁶The righteous will see it and be amazed.
    They will laugh and say,
⁷"Look what happens to mighty warriors
    who do not trust in God.
They trust their wealth instead
    and grow more and more bold in their wickedness."

⁸But I am like an olive tree,
    thriving in the house of God.
I trust in God's unfailing love
    forever and ever.
⁹I will praise you forever, O God,
    for what you have done.
I will wait for your mercies
    in the presence of your people.

PSALM 53

For the choir director: A meditation of David.

¹Only fools say in their hearts,
  "There is no God."
They are corrupt, and their actions are evil;
  no one does good!

²God looks down from heaven
  on the entire human race;
he looks to see if there is even one with real
      understanding,
  one who seeks for God.
³But no, all have turned away from God;
  all have become corrupt.
No one does good,
  not even one!

⁴Will those who do evil never learn?
  They eat up my people like bread;
  they wouldn't think of praying to God.
⁵But then terror will grip them,
  terror like they have never known before.
God will scatter the bones of your enemies.
  You will put them to shame, for God has rejected
      them.

⁶Oh, that salvation would come from Mount Zion to
        rescue Israel!
    For when God restores his people,
    Jacob will shout with joy, and Israel will rejoice.

PSALM 54

*For the choir director: A meditation of David, regarding the time the
Ziphites came and said to Saul, "We know where David is hiding." To be
accompanied by stringed instruments.*

¹Come with great power, O God, and rescue me!
    Defend me with your might.
²O God, listen to my prayer.
    Pay attention to my plea.

³For strangers are attacking me;
    violent men are trying to kill me.
    They care nothing for God.   *Interlude*

⁴But God is my helper.
    The Lord is the one who keeps me alive!
⁵May my enemies' plans for evil be turned against them.
    Do as you promised and put an end to them.

⁶I will sacrifice a voluntary offering to you;
    I will praise your name, O LORD,
        for it is good.

⁷For you will rescue me from my troubles
    and help me to triumph over my enemies.

PSALM 55

For the choir director: A psalm of David, to be accompanied by stringed instruments.

¹Listen to my prayer, O God.
    Do not ignore my cry for help!
²Please listen and answer me,
    for I am overwhelmed by my troubles.
³My enemies shout at me,
    making loud and wicked threats.
They bring trouble on me,
    hunting me down in their anger.

⁴My heart is in anguish.
    The terror of death overpowers me.
⁵Fear and trembling overwhelm me.
    I can't stop shaking.
⁶Oh, how I wish I had wings like a dove;
    then I would fly away and rest!
⁷I would fly far away
    to the quiet of the wilderness.   *Interlude*

⁸How quickly I would escape—
   far away from this wild storm of hatred.

⁹Destroy them, Lord, and confuse their speech,
   for I see violence and strife in the city.
¹⁰Its walls are patrolled day and night against invaders,
   but the real danger is wickedness within the city.
¹¹Murder and robbery are everywhere there;
   threats and cheating are rampant in the streets.

¹²It is not an enemy who taunts me—
   I could bear that.
It is not my foes who so arrogantly insult me—
   I could have hidden from them.
¹³Instead, it is you—my equal,
   my companion and close friend.
¹⁴What good fellowship we enjoyed
   as we walked together to the house of God.

¹⁵Let death seize my enemies by surprise;
   let the grave swallow them alive,
   for evil makes its home within them.

¹⁶But I will call on God,
   and the LORD will rescue me.

¹⁷Morning, noon, and night
    I plead aloud in my distress,
    and the LORD hears my voice.
¹⁸He rescues me and keeps me safe
    from the battle waged against me,
    even though many still oppose me.
¹⁹God, who is king forever,
    will hear me and will humble them.   *Interlude*
For my enemies refuse to change their ways;
    they do not fear God.

²⁰As for this friend of mine, he betrayed me;
    he broke his promises.
²¹His words are as smooth as cream,
    but in his heart is war.
His words are as soothing as lotion,
    but underneath are daggers!

²²Give your burdens to the LORD,
    and he will take care of you.
    He will not permit the godly to slip and fall.

²³But you, O God, will send the wicked
    down to the pit of destruction.
Murderers and liars will die young,
    but I am trusting you to save me.

The LORD hates cheating, but he delights in honesty.

²Pride leads to disgrace, but with humility comes wisdom.

³Good people are guided by their honesty; treacherous people are destroyed by their dishonesty.

⁴Riches won't help on the day of judgment, but right living is a safeguard against death.

⁵The godly are directed by their honesty; the wicked fall beneath their load of sin.

⁶The godliness of good people rescues them; the ambition of treacherous people traps them.

⁷When the wicked die, their hopes all perish, for they rely on their own feeble strength.

⁸God rescues the godly from danger, but he lets the wicked fall into trouble.

⁹Evil words destroy one's friends; wise discernment rescues the godly.

¹⁰The whole city celebrates when the godly succeed; they shout for joy when the godless die.

¹¹Upright citizens bless a city and make it prosper, but the talk of the wicked tears it apart.

¹²It is foolish to belittle a neighbor; a person with good sense remains silent.

¹³A gossip goes around revealing secrets, but those who are trustworthy can keep a confidence.

¹⁴Without wise leadership, a nation falls; with many counselors, there is safety.

¹⁵Guaranteeing a loan for a stranger is dangerous; it is better to refuse than to suffer later.

¹⁶Beautiful women obtain wealth, and violent men get rich.

¹⁷Your own soul is nourished when you are kind, but you destroy yourself when you are cruel.

¹⁸Evil people get rich for the moment, but the reward of the godly will last.

¹⁹Godly people find life; evil people find death.

²⁰The LORD hates people with twisted hearts, but he delights in those who have integrity.

²¹You can be sure that evil people will be punished, but the children of the godly will go free.

²²A woman who is beautiful but lacks discretion is like a gold ring in a pig's snout.

²³The godly can look forward to happiness, while the wicked can expect only wrath.

²⁴It is possible to give freely and become more wealthy, but those who are stingy will lose everything.

²⁵The generous prosper and are satisfied; those who refresh others will themselves be refreshed.

²⁶People curse those who hold their grain for higher prices, but they bless the one who sells to them in their time of need.

²⁷If you search for good, you will find favor; but if you search for evil, it will find you!

²⁸Trust in your money and down you go! But the godly flourish like leaves in spring.

²⁹Those who bring trouble on their families inherit only the wind. The fool will be a servant to the wise.

³⁰The godly are like trees that bear life-giving fruit, and those who save lives are wise.

³¹If the righteous are rewarded here on earth, how much more true that the wicked and the sinner will get what they deserve!

DAY TWELVE

P SALM 56

For the choir director: A psalm of David, regarding the time the
Philistines seized him in Gath. To be sung to the tune "Dove on
Distant Oaks."

¹O God, have mercy on me.
  The enemy troops press in on me.
  My foes attack me all day long.
²My slanderers hound me constantly,
  and many are boldly attacking me.
³But when I am afraid,
  I put my trust in you.
⁴O God, I praise your word.
  I trust in God, so why should I be afraid?
  What can mere mortals do to me?

⁵They are always twisting what I say;
  they spend their days plotting ways to harm me.
⁶They come together to spy on me—
  watching my every step, eager to kill me.

⁷Don't let them get away with their wickedness;
    in your anger, O God, throw them to the ground.

⁸You keep track of all my sorrows.
    You have collected all my tears in your bottle.
    You have recorded each one in your book.

⁹On the very day I call to you for help,
    my enemies will retreat.
    This I know: God is on my side.
¹⁰O God, I praise your word.
    Yes, LORD, I praise your word.
¹¹I trust in God, so why should I be afraid?
    What can mere mortals do to me?

¹²I will fulfill my vows to you, O God,
    and offer a sacrifice of thanks for your help.
¹³For you have rescued me from death;
    you have kept my feet from slipping.
So now I can walk in your presence, O God,
    in your life-giving light.

PSALM 57

For the choir director: A psalm of David, regarding the time he fled from Saul and went into the cave. To be sung to the tune "Do Not Destroy!"

¹Have mercy on me, O God, have mercy!
    I look to you for protection.
I will hide beneath the shadow of your wings
    until this violent storm is past.

²I cry out to God Most High,
    to God who will fulfill his purpose for me.
³He will send help from heaven to save me,
    rescuing me from those who are out to get me.

                        Interlude
My God will send forth his unfailing love and faithfulness.

⁴I am surrounded by fierce lions
    who greedily devour human prey—
whose teeth pierce like spears and arrows,
    and whose tongues cut like swords.

⁵Be exalted, O God, above the highest heavens!
    May your glory shine over all the earth.

⁶My enemies have set a trap for me.
    I am weary from distress.
They have dug a deep pit in my path,
    but they themselves have fallen into it.   *Interlude*

⁷My heart is confident in you, O God;
    no wonder I can sing your praises!

[8]Wake up, my soul!

    Wake up, O harp and lyre!

    I will waken the dawn with my song.

[9]I will thank you, Lord, in front of all the people.

    I will sing your praises among the nations.

[10]For your unfailing love is as high as the heavens.

    Your faithfulness reaches to the clouds.

[11]Be exalted, O God, above the highest heavens.

    May your glory shine over all the earth.

PSALM 58

For the choir director: A psalm of David, to be sung to the tune "Do Not Destroy!"

[1]Justice—do you rulers know the meaning of the word?

    Do you judge the people fairly?

[2]No, all your dealings are crooked;

    you hand out violence instead of justice.

[3]These wicked people are born sinners;

    even from birth they have lied and gone their own way.

[4]They spit poison like deadly snakes;

    they are like cobras that refuse to listen,

⁵ignoring the tunes of the snake charmers,
no matter how skillfully they play.

⁶Break off their fangs, O God!
Smash the jaws of these lions, O LORD!
⁷May they disappear like water into thirsty ground.
Make their weapons useless in their hands.
⁸May they be like snails that dissolve into slime,
like a stillborn child who will never see the sun.
⁹God will sweep them away, both young and old,
faster than a pot heats on an open flame.

¹⁰The godly will rejoice when they see injustice avenged.
They will wash their feet in the blood of the wicked.
¹¹Then at last everyone will say,
"There truly is a reward for those who live for God;
surely there is a God who judges justly here on
earth."

PSALM 59

*For the choir director: A psalm of David, regarding the time Saul sent
soldiers to watch David's house in order to kill him. To be sung to the
tune "Do Not Destroy!"*

¹Rescue me from my enemies, O God.
Protect me from those who have come to destroy me.

²Rescue me from these criminals;

    save me from these murderers.

³They have set an ambush for me.

    Fierce enemies are out there waiting,

    though I have done them no wrong, O LORD.

⁴Despite my innocence, they prepare to kill me.

    Rise up and help me! Look on my plight!

⁵O LORD God Almighty, the God of Israel,

    rise up to punish hostile nations.

    Show no mercy to wicked traitors.   *Interlude*

⁶They come at night,

    snarling like vicious dogs

    as they prowl the streets.

⁷Listen to the filth that comes from their mouths,

    the piercing swords that fly from their lips.

    "Who can hurt us?" they sneer.

⁸But LORD, you laugh at them.

    You scoff at all the hostile nations.

⁹You are my strength; I wait for you to rescue me,

    for you, O God, are my place of safety.

¹⁰In his unfailing love, my God will come and help me.

    He will let me look down in triumph on all my

        enemies.

¹¹Don't kill them, for my people soon forget such
        lessons;
    stagger them with your power, and bring them to
        their knees,
    O Lord our shield.
¹²Because of the sinful things they say,
    because of the evil that is on their lips,
let them be captured by their pride,
    their curses, and their lies.
¹³Destroy them in your anger!
    Wipe them out completely!
Then the whole world will know
    that God reigns in Israel.   *Interlude*

¹⁴My enemies come out at night,
    snarling like vicious dogs
    as they prowl the streets.
¹⁵They scavenge for food
    but go to sleep unsatisfied.

¹⁶But as for me, I will sing about your power.
    I will shout with joy each morning because of your
        unfailing love.
For you have been my refuge,
    a place of safety in the day of distress.

¹⁷O my Strength, to you I sing praises,
for you, O God, are my refuge,
the God who shows me unfailing love.

PSALM 60

For the choir director: A psalm of David useful for teaching, regarding the time David fought Aram-naharaim and Aram-zobah, and Joab returned and killed twelve thousand Edomites in the Valley of Salt. To be sung to the tune "Lily of the Testimony."

¹You have rejected us, O God, and broken our defenses.
You have been angry with us; now restore us to your
favor.
²You have shaken our land and split it open.
Seal the cracks before it completely collapses.
³You have been very hard on us,
making us drink wine that sent us reeling.
⁴But you have raised a banner for those who honor you—
a rallying point in the face of attack.   *Interlude*

⁵Use your strong right arm to save us,
and rescue your beloved people.
⁶God has promised this by his holiness:
"I will divide up Shechem with joy.
I will measure out the valley of Succoth.

⁷Gilead is mine,
 and Manasseh is mine.
Ephraim will produce my warriors,
 and Judah will produce my kings.
 ⁸Moab will become my lowly servant,
 and Edom will be my slave.
 I will shout in triumph over the Philistines."

⁹But who will bring me into the fortified city?
 Who will bring me victory over Edom?
¹⁰Have you rejected us, O God?
 Will you no longer march with our armies?
¹¹Oh, please help us against our enemies,
 for all human help is useless.
¹²With God's help we will do mighty things,
 for he will trample down our foes.

PROVERBS 12

To learn, you must love discipline; it is stupid to hate correction.

²The LORD approves of those who are good, but he condemns those who plan wickedness.

³Wickedness never brings stability; only the godly have deep roots.

⁴A worthy wife is her husband's joy and crown; a shameful wife saps his strength.

⁵The plans of the godly are just; the advice of the wicked is treacherous.

⁶The words of the wicked are like a murderous ambush, but the words of the godly save lives.

⁷The wicked perish and are gone, but the children of the godly stand firm.

⁸Everyone admires a person with good sense, but a warped mind is despised.

⁹It is better to be a nobody with a servant than to be self-important but have no food.

¹⁰The godly are concerned for the welfare of their animals, but even the kindness of the wicked is cruel.

¹¹Hard work means prosperity; only fools idle away their time.

¹²Thieves are jealous of each other's loot, while the godly bear their own fruit.

¹³The wicked are trapped by their own words, but the godly escape such trouble.

¹⁴People can get many good things by the words they say; the work of their hands also gives them many benefits.

¹⁵Fools think they need no advice, but the wise listen to others.

¹⁶A fool is quick-tempered, but a wise person stays calm when insulted.

¹⁷An honest witness tells the truth; a false witness tells lies.

¹⁸Some people make cutting remarks, but the words of the wise bring healing.

¹⁹Truth stands the test of time; lies are soon exposed.

²⁰Deceit fills hearts that are plotting evil; joy fills hearts that are planning peace!

²¹No real harm befalls the godly, but the wicked have their fill of trouble.

²²The LORD hates those who don't keep their word, but he delights in those who do.

²³Wise people don't make a show of their knowledge, but fools broadcast their folly.

²⁴Work hard and become a leader; be lazy and become a slave.

²⁵Worry weighs a person down; an encouraging word cheers a person up.

²⁶The godly give good advice to their friends; the wicked lead them astray.

²⁷Lazy people don't even cook the game they catch, but the diligent make use of everything they find.

²⁸The way of the godly leads to life; their path does not lead to death.

DAY THIRTEEN

P SALM 61

*For the choir director: A psalm of David, to be accompanied by stringed
instruments.*

¹O God, listen to my cry!
  Hear my prayer!
²From the ends of the earth,
  I will cry to you for help,
  for my heart is overwhelmed.
Lead me to the towering rock of safety,
³   for you are my safe refuge,
  a fortress where my enemies cannot reach me.
⁴Let me live forever in your sanctuary,
  safe beneath the shelter of your wings!   *Interlude*
⁵For you have heard my vows, O God.
  You have given me an inheritance reserved for those
    who fear your name.

⁶Add many years to the life of the king!
  May his years span the generations!

⁷May he reign under God's protection forever.
Appoint your unfailing love and faithfulness to watch
over him.

⁸Then I will always sing praises to your name
as I fulfill my vows day after day.

PSALM 62

For Jeduthun, the choir director: A psalm of David.

¹I wait quietly before God,
for my salvation comes from him.
²He alone is my rock and my salvation,
my fortress where I will never be shaken.

³So many enemies against one man—
all of them trying to kill me.
To them I'm just a broken-down wall
or a tottering fence.
⁴They plan to topple me from my high position.
They delight in telling lies about me.
They are friendly to my face,
but they curse me in their hearts. *Interlude*

⁵I wait quietly before God,
for my hope is in him.

⁶He alone is my rock and my salvation,
>   my fortress where I will not be shaken.
⁷My salvation and my honor come from God alone.
>   He is my refuge, a rock where no enemy can reach me.

⁸O my people, trust in him at all times.
>   Pour out your heart to him,
>   for God is our refuge.   *Interlude*

⁹From the greatest to the lowliest—
>   all are nothing in his sight.
If you weigh them on the scales,
>   they are lighter than a puff of air.
¹⁰Don't try to get rich
>   by extortion or robbery.
And if your wealth increases,
>   don't make it the center of your life.

¹¹God has spoken plainly,
>   and I have heard it many times:
Power, O God, belongs to you;
¹²   unfailing love, O Lord, is yours.
Surely you judge all people
>   according to what they have done.

PSALM 63

A psalm of David, regarding a time when David was in the wilderness of Judah.

¹O God, you are my God;
    I earnestly search for you.
My soul thirsts for you;
    my whole body longs for you
in this parched and weary land
    where there is no water.

²I have seen you in your sanctuary
    and gazed upon your power and glory.
³Your unfailing love is better to me than life itself;
    how I praise you!
⁴I will honor you as long as I live,
    lifting up my hands to you in prayer.
⁵You satisfy me more than the richest of foods.
    I will praise you with songs of joy.

⁶I lie awake thinking of you,
    meditating on you through the night.
⁷I think how much you have helped me;
    I sing for joy in the shadow of your protecting wings.
⁸I follow close behind you;
    your strong right hand holds me securely.

⁹But those plotting to destroy me will come to ruin.
  They will go down into the depths of the earth.
¹⁰They will die by the sword
  and become the food of jackals.

¹¹But the king will rejoice in God.
  All who trust in him will praise him,
  while liars will be silenced.

PSALM 64

For the choir director: A psalm of David.

¹O God, listen to my complaint.
  Do not let my enemies' threats overwhelm me.
²Protect me from the plots of the wicked,
  from the scheming of those who do evil.
³Sharp tongues are the swords they wield;
  bitter words are the arrows they aim.
⁴They shoot from ambush at the innocent,
  attacking suddenly and fearlessly.
⁵They encourage each other to do evil
  and plan how to set their traps.
  "Who will ever notice?" they ask.
⁶As they plot their crimes, they say,
  "We have devised the perfect plan!"

Yes, the human heart and mind are cunning.

⁷But God himself will shoot them down.
　　Suddenly, his arrows will pierce them.
⁸Their own words will be turned against them, destroying
　　　them.
　　All who see it happening will shake their heads in
　　　scorn.
⁹Then everyone will stand in awe,
　　proclaiming the mighty acts of God,
　　realizing all the amazing things he does.

¹⁰The godly will rejoice in the LORD
　　and find shelter in him.
And those who do what is right
　　will praise him.

PSALM 65　

For the choir director: A psalm of David. A song.

¹What mighty praise, O God,
　　belongs to you in Zion.
We will fulfill our vows to you,
² 　for you answer our prayers,
　　and to you all people will come.

³Though our hearts are filled with sins,
    you forgive them all.
⁴What joy for those you choose to bring near,
    those who live in your holy courts.
What joys await us
    inside your holy Temple.

⁵You faithfully answer our prayers with awesome
        deeds,
    O God our savior.
You are the hope of everyone on earth,
    even those who sail on distant seas.
⁶You formed the mountains by your power
    and armed yourself with mighty strength.
⁷You quieted the raging oceans
    with their pounding waves
    and silenced the shouting of the nations.
⁸Those who live at the ends of the earth
    stand in awe of your wonders.
From where the sun rises to where it sets,
    you inspire shouts of joy.

⁹You take care of the earth and water it,
    making it rich and fertile.
The rivers of God will not run dry;

they provide a bountiful harvest of grain,
    for you have ordered it so.
[10]You drench the plowed ground with rain,
    melting the clods and leveling the ridges.
You soften the earth with showers
    and bless its abundant crops.
[11]You crown the year with a bountiful harvest;
    even the hard pathways overflow with abundance.
[12]The wilderness becomes a lush pasture,
    and the hillsides blossom with joy.
[13]The meadows are clothed with flocks of sheep,
    and the valleys are carpeted with grain.
    They all shout and sing for joy!

PROVERBS 13

A wise child accepts a parent's discipline; a young mocker refuses to listen.

[2]Good people enjoy the positive results of their words, but those who are treacherous crave violence.

[3]Those who control their tongue will have a long life; a quick retort can ruin everything.

[4]Lazy people want much but get little, but those who work hard will prosper and be satisfied.

⁵Those who are godly hate lies; the wicked come to shame and disgrace.

⁶Godliness helps people all through life, while the evil are destroyed by their wickedness.

⁷Some who are poor pretend to be rich; others who are rich pretend to be poor.

⁸The rich can pay a ransom, but the poor won't even get threatened.

⁹The life of the godly is full of light and joy, but the sinner's light is snuffed out.

¹⁰Pride leads to arguments; those who take advice are wise.

¹¹Wealth from get-rich-quick schemes quickly disappears; wealth from hard work grows.

¹²Hope deferred makes the heart sick, but when dreams come true, there is life and joy.

¹³People who despise advice will find themselves in trouble; those who respect it will succeed.

¹⁴The advice of the wise is like a life-giving fountain; those who accept it avoid the snares of death.

¹⁵A person with good sense is respected; a treacherous person walks a rocky road.

¹⁶Wise people think before they act; fools don't and even brag about it!

¹⁷An unreliable messenger stumbles into trouble, but a reliable messenger brings healing.

¹⁸If you ignore criticism, you will end in poverty and disgrace; if you accept criticism, you will be honored.

¹⁹It is pleasant to see dreams come true, but fools will not turn from evil to attain them.

²⁰Whoever walks with the wise will become wise; whoever walks with fools will suffer harm.

²¹Trouble chases sinners, while blessings chase the righteous!

²²Good people leave an inheritance to their grandchildren, but the sinner's wealth passes to the godly.

²³A poor person's farm may produce much food, but injustice sweeps it all away.

²⁴If you refuse to discipline your children, it proves you don't love them; if you love your children, you will be prompt to discipline them.

²⁵The godly eat to their hearts' content, but the belly of the wicked goes hungry.

DAY FOURTEEN

P SALM 66

For the choir director: A psalm. A song.

¹Shout joyful praises to God, all the earth!
² Sing about the glory of his name!
Tell the world how glorious he is.
³Say to God, "How awesome are your deeds!
Your enemies cringe before your mighty power.
⁴Everything on earth will worship you;
they will sing your praises,
shouting your name in glorious songs."   *Interlude*

⁵Come and see what our God has done,
what awesome miracles he does for his people!
⁶He made a dry path through the Red Sea,
and his people went across on foot.
Come, let us rejoice in who he is.
⁷For by his great power he rules forever.
He watches every movement of the nations;
let no rebel rise in defiance.   *Interlude*

⁸Let the whole world bless our God
   and sing aloud his praises.
⁹Our lives are in his hands,
   and he keeps our feet from stumbling.
¹⁰You have tested us, O God;
   you have purified us like silver melted in a crucible.
¹¹You captured us in your net
   and laid the burden of slavery on our backs.
¹²You sent troops to ride across our broken bodies.
   We went through fire and flood.
   But you brought us to a place of great abundance.

¹³Now I come to your Temple with burnt offerings
   to fulfill the vows I made to you—
¹⁴yes, the sacred vows you heard me make
   when I was in deep trouble.
¹⁵That is why I am sacrificing burnt offerings to you—
   the best of my rams as a pleasing aroma.
   And I will sacrifice bulls and goats.   *Interlude*

¹⁶Come and listen, all you who fear God,
   and I will tell you what he did for me.
¹⁷For I cried out to him for help,
   praising him as I spoke.
¹⁸If I had not confessed the sin in my heart,
   my Lord would not have listened.

[19]But God did listen!
>He paid attention to my prayer.

[20]Praise God, who did not ignore my prayer
>and did not withdraw his unfailing love from me.

PSALM 67

*For the choir director: A psalm, to be accompanied by stringed
instruments. A song.*

[1]May God be merciful and bless us.
>May his face shine with favor upon us.   *Interlude*

[2]May your ways be known throughout the earth,
>your saving power among people everywhere.

[3]May the nations praise you, O God.
>Yes, may all the nations praise you.

[4]How glad the nations will be, singing for joy,
>because you govern them with justice
>and direct the actions of the whole world.   *Interlude*

[5]May the nations praise you, O God.
>Yes, may all the nations praise you.

[6]Then the earth will yield its harvests,
>and God, our God, will richly bless us.

[7]Yes, God will bless us,
>and people all over the world will fear him.

PSALM 68

For the choir director: A psalm of David. A song.

¹Arise, O God, and scatter your enemies.
  Let those who hate God run for their lives.
²Drive them off like smoke blown by the wind.
  Melt them like wax in fire.
  Let the wicked perish in the presence of God.
³But let the godly rejoice.
  Let them be glad in God's presence.
  Let them be filled with joy.

⁴Sing praises to God and to his name!
  Sing loud praises to him who rides the clouds.
His name is the LORD—
  rejoice in his presence!

⁵Father to the fatherless, defender of widows—
  this is God, whose dwelling is holy.
⁶God places the lonely in families;
  he sets the prisoners free and gives them joy.
  But for rebels, there is only famine and distress.

⁷O God, when you led your people from Egypt,
  when you marched through the wilderness,   *Interlude*
⁸the earth trembled, and the heavens poured rain

before you, the God of Sinai,
    before God, the God of Israel.
⁹You sent abundant rain, O God,
    to refresh the weary Promised Land.
¹⁰There your people finally settled,
    and with a bountiful harvest, O God,
    you provided for your needy people.

¹¹The Lord announces victory,
    and throngs of women shout the happy news.
¹²Enemy kings and their armies flee,
    while the women of Israel divide the plunder.
¹³Though they lived among the sheepfolds,
    now they are covered with silver and gold,
    as a dove is covered by its wings.
¹⁴The Almighty scattered the enemy kings
    like a blowing snowstorm on Mount Zalmon.

¹⁵The majestic mountains of Bashan
    stretch high into the sky.
¹⁶Why do you look with envy, O rugged mountains,
    at Mount Zion, where God has chosen to live,
    where the LORD himself will live forever?

¹⁷Surrounded by unnumbered thousands of chariots,
    the Lord came from Mount Sinai into his sanctuary.

¹⁸When you ascended to the heights,
    you led a crowd of captives.
You received gifts from the people,
    even from those who rebelled against you.
    Now the LORD God will live among us here.

¹⁹Praise the Lord; praise God our savior!
    For each day he carries us in his arms.   *Interlude*
²⁰Our God is a God who saves!
    The Sovereign LORD rescues us from death.

²¹But God will smash the heads of his enemies,
    crushing the skulls of those who love their guilty
        ways.
²²The Lord says, "I will bring my enemies down from
        Bashan;
    I will bring them up from the depths of the sea.
²³You, my people, will wash your feet in their blood,
    and even your dogs will get their share!"

²⁴Your procession has come into view, O God—
    the procession of my God and King
    as he goes into the sanctuary.
²⁵Singers are in front, musicians are behind;
    with them are young women playing tambourines.

²⁶Praise God, all you people of Israel;
>   praise the Lord, the source of Israel's life.
²⁷Look, the little tribe of Benjamin leads the way.
>   Then comes a great throng of rulers from Judah
>   and all the rulers of Zebulun and Naphtali.

²⁸Summon your might, O God.
>   Display your power, O God, as you have in the past.
²⁹The kings of the earth are bringing tribute
>   to your Temple in Jerusalem.
³⁰Rebuke these enemy nations—
>   these wild animals lurking in the reeds,
>   this herd of bulls among the weaker calves.
Humble those who demand tribute from us.
>   Scatter the nations that delight in war.
³¹Let Egypt come with gifts of precious metals;
>   let Ethiopia bow in submission to God.
³²Sing to God, you kingdoms of the earth.
>   Sing praises to the Lord.   *Interlude*

³³Sing to the one who rides across the ancient heavens,
>   his mighty voice thundering from the sky.
³⁴Tell everyone about God's power.
>   His majesty shines down on Israel;
>   his strength is mighty in the heavens.

³⁵God is awesome in his sanctuary.

> The God of Israel gives power and strength to his
> people.

Praise be to God!

PSALM 69

For the choir director: A psalm of David, to be sung to the tune
"Lilies."

¹Save me, O God,

> for the floodwaters are up to my neck.

²Deeper and deeper I sink into the mire;

> I can't find a foothold to stand on.

I am in deep water,

> and the floods overwhelm me.

³I am exhausted from crying for help;

> my throat is parched and dry.

My eyes are swollen with weeping,

> waiting for my God to help me.

⁴Those who hate me without cause

> are more numerous than the hairs on my head.

These enemies who seek to destroy me

> are doing so without cause.

They attack me with lies,
    demanding that I give back what I didn't steal.

⁵O God, you know how foolish I am;
    my sins cannot be hidden from you.
⁶Don't let those who trust in you stumble because of me,
    O Sovereign LORD Almighty.
Don't let me cause them to be humiliated,
    O God of Israel.
⁷For I am mocked and shamed for your sake;
    humiliation is written all over my face.
⁸Even my own brothers pretend they don't know me;
    they treat me like a stranger.

⁹Passion for your house burns within me,
    so those who insult you are also insulting me.
¹⁰When I weep and fast before the LORD,
    they scoff at me.
¹¹When I dress in sackcloth to show sorrow,
    they make fun of me.
¹²I am the favorite topic of town gossip,
    and all the drunkards sing about me.

¹³But I keep right on praying to you, LORD,
    hoping this is the time you will show me favor.

In your unfailing love, O God,
    answer my prayer with your sure salvation.
¹⁴Pull me out of the mud;
    don't let me sink any deeper!
Rescue me from those who hate me,
    and pull me from these deep waters.
¹⁵Don't let the floods overwhelm me,
    or the deep waters swallow me,
    or the pit of death devour me.

¹⁶Answer my prayers, O LORD,
    for your unfailing love is wonderful.
Turn and take care of me,
    for your mercy is so plentiful.
¹⁷Don't hide from your servant;
    answer me quickly, for I am in deep trouble!
¹⁸Come and rescue me;
    free me from all my enemies.

¹⁹You know the insults I endure—
    the humiliation and disgrace.
You have seen all my enemies
    and know what they have said.
²⁰Their insults have broken my heart,
    and I am in despair.

If only one person would show some pity;
    if only one would turn and comfort me.
²¹But instead, they give me poison for food;
    they offer me sour wine to satisfy my thirst.

²²Let the bountiful table set before them become a snare,
    and let their security become a trap.
²³Let their eyes go blind so they cannot see,
    and let their bodies grow weaker and weaker.
²⁴Pour out your fury on them;
    consume them with your burning anger.
²⁵May their homes become desolate
    and their tents be deserted.
²⁶To those you have punished, they add insult to injury;
    they scoff at the pain of those you have hurt.
²⁷Pile their sins up high,
    and don't let them go free.
²⁸Erase their names from the Book of Life;
    don't let them be counted among the righteous.

²⁹I am suffering and in pain.
    Rescue me, O God, by your saving power.

³⁰Then I will praise God's name with singing,
    and I will honor him with thanksgiving.

³¹For this will please the LORD more than sacrificing an ox
   or presenting a bull with its horns and hooves.
³²The humble will see their God at work and be glad.
   Let all who seek God's help live in joy.
³³For the LORD hears the cries of his needy ones;
   he does not despise his people who are oppressed.

³⁴Praise him, O heaven and earth,
   the seas and all that move in them.
³⁵For God will save Jerusalem
   and rebuild the towns of Judah.
His people will live there
   and take possession of the land.
³⁶The descendants of those who obey him will inherit the
   land,
   and those who love him will live there in safety.

PSALM 70

*For the choir director: A psalm of David, to bring us to the LORD's
remembrance.*

¹Please, God, rescue me!
   Come quickly, LORD, and help me.
²May those who try to destroy me
   be humiliated and put to shame.

May those who take delight in my trouble
    be turned back in disgrace.
³Let them be horrified by their shame,
    for they said, "Aha! We've got him now!"
⁴But may all who search for you
    be filled with joy and gladness.
May those who love your salvation
    repeatedly shout, "God is great!"
⁵But I am poor and needy;
    please hurry to my aid, O God.
You are my helper and my savior;
    O LORD, do not delay!

PROVERBS 14

A wise woman builds her house; a foolish woman tears
hers down with her own hands.

²Those who follow the right path fear the LORD; those
who take the wrong path despise him.

³The talk of fools is a rod for their backs, but the
words of the wise keep them out of trouble.

⁴An empty stable stays clean, but no income comes
from an empty stable.

⁵A truthful witness does not lie; a false witness
breathes lies.

⁶A mocker seeks wisdom and never finds it, but knowledge comes easily to those with understanding.

⁷Stay away from fools, for you won't find knowledge there.

⁸The wise look ahead to see what is coming, but fools deceive themselves.

⁹Fools make fun of guilt, but the godly acknowledge it and seek reconciliation.

¹⁰Each heart knows its own bitterness, and no one else can fully share its joy.

¹¹The house of the wicked will perish, but the tent of the godly will flourish.

¹²There is a path before each person that seems right, but it ends in death.

¹³Laughter can conceal a heavy heart; when the laughter ends, the grief remains.

¹⁴Backsliders get what they deserve; good people receive their reward.

¹⁵Only simpletons believe everything they are told! The prudent carefully consider their steps.

¹⁶The wise are cautious and avoid danger; fools plunge ahead with great confidence.

¹⁷Those who are short-tempered do foolish things, and schemers are hated.

¹⁸The simpleton is clothed with folly, but the wise person is crowned with knowledge.

¹⁹Evil people will bow before good people; the wicked will bow at the gates of the godly.

²⁰The poor are despised even by their neighbors, while the rich have many "friends."

²¹It is sin to despise one's neighbors; blessed are those who help the poor.

²²If you plot evil, you will be lost; but if you plan good, you will be granted unfailing love and faithfulness.

²³Work brings profit, but mere talk leads to poverty!

²⁴Wealth is a crown for the wise; the effort of fools yields only folly.

²⁵A truthful witness saves lives, but a false witness is a traitor.

²⁶Those who fear the LORD are secure; he will be a place of refuge for their children.

²⁷Fear of the LORD is a life-giving fountain; it offers escape from the snares of death.

²⁸A growing population is a king's glory; a dwindling nation is his doom.

²⁹Those who control their anger have great understanding; those with a hasty temper will make mistakes.

[30]A relaxed attitude lengthens life; jealousy rots it away.

[31]Those who oppress the poor insult their Maker, but those who help the poor honor him.

[32]The wicked are crushed by their sins, but the godly have a refuge when they die.

[33]Wisdom is enshrined in an understanding heart; wisdom is not found among fools.

[34]Godliness exalts a nation, but sin is a disgrace to any people.

[35]A king rejoices in servants who know what they are doing; he is angry with those who cause trouble.

DAY FIFTEEN

PSALM 71

¹O LORD, you are my refuge;
    never let me be disgraced.
²Rescue me! Save me from my enemies, for you are just.
    Turn your ear to listen and set me free.
³Be to me a protecting rock of safety,
    where I am always welcome.
Give the order to save me,
    for you are my rock and my fortress.

⁴My God, rescue me from the power of the wicked,
    from the clutches of cruel oppressors.
⁵O Lord, you alone are my hope.
    I've trusted you, O LORD, from childhood.
⁶Yes, you have been with me from birth;
    from my mother's womb you have cared for me.
No wonder I am always praising you!

⁷My life is an example to many,
    because you have been my strength and protection.

⁸That is why I can never stop praising you;
    I declare your glory all day long.

⁹And now, in my old age, don't set me aside.
    Don't abandon me when my strength is failing.
¹⁰For my enemies are whispering against me.
    They are plotting together to kill me.
¹¹They say, "God has abandoned him.
    Let's go and get him,
      for there is no one to help him now."

¹²O God, don't stay away.
    My God, please hurry to help me.
¹³Bring disgrace and destruction on those who accuse me.
    May humiliation and shame cover
    those who want to harm me.

¹⁴But I will keep on hoping for you to help me;
    I will praise you more and more.
¹⁵I will tell everyone about your righteousness.
    All day long I will proclaim your saving power,
      for I am overwhelmed by how much you have done
        for me.
¹⁶I will praise your mighty deeds, O Sovereign LORD.
    I will tell everyone that you alone are just and good.

¹⁷O God, you have taught me from my earliest childhood,
   and I have constantly told others about the wonderful
      things you do.
¹⁸Now that I am old and gray,
   do not abandon me, O God.
Let me proclaim your power to this new generation,
   your mighty miracles to all who come after me.

¹⁹Your righteousness, O God, reaches to the highest heavens.
   You have done such wonderful things.
   Who can compare with you, O God?
²⁰You have allowed me to suffer much hardship,
   but you will restore me to life again
   and lift me up from the depths of the earth.
²¹You will restore me to even greater honor
   and comfort me once again.

²²Then I will praise you with music on the harp,
   because you are faithful to your promises, O God.
I will sing for you with a lyre,
   O Holy One of Israel.
²³I will shout for joy and sing your praises,
   for you have redeemed me.
²⁴I will tell about your righteous deeds
   all day long,

for everyone who tried to hurt me
  has been shamed and humiliated.

PSALM 72

A psalm of Solomon.

¹Give justice to the king, O God,
  and righteousness to the king's son.
²Help him judge your people in the right way;
  let the poor always be treated fairly.
³May the mountains yield prosperity for all,
  and may the hills be fruitful,
  because the king does what is right.
⁴Help him to defend the poor,
  to rescue the children of the needy,
  and to crush their oppressors.
⁵May he live as long as the sun shines,
  as long as the moon continues in the skies.
  Yes, forever!
⁶May his reign be as refreshing as the springtime rains—
  like the showers that water the earth.
⁷May all the godly flourish during his reign.
  May there be abundant prosperity until the end of
    time.

⁸May he reign from sea to sea,
    and from the Euphrates River to the ends of the earth.
⁹Desert nomads will bow before him;
    his enemies will fall before him in the dust.
¹⁰The western kings of Tarshish and the islands
    will bring him tribute.
The eastern kings of Sheba and Seba
    will bring him gifts.
¹¹All kings will bow before him,
    and all nations will serve him.

¹²He will rescue the poor when they cry to him;
    he will help the oppressed, who have no one to
        defend them.
¹³He feels pity for the weak and the needy,
    and he will rescue them.
¹⁴He will save them from oppression and from violence,
    for their lives are precious to him.

¹⁵Long live the king!
    May the gold of Sheba be given to him.
May the people always pray for him
    and bless him all day long.
¹⁶May there be abundant crops throughout the land,
    flourishing even on the mountaintops.

May the fruit trees flourish as they do in Lebanon,
     sprouting up like grass in a field.
¹⁷May the king's name endure forever;
     may it continue as long as the sun shines.
May all nations be blessed through him
     and bring him praise.

¹⁸Bless the LORD God, the God of Israel,
     who alone does such wonderful things.
¹⁹Bless his glorious name forever!
     Let the whole earth be filled with his glory.
     Amen and amen!

²⁰(This ends the prayers of David son of Jesse.)

BOOK THREE (Psalms 73–89)

PSALM 7 3

A psalm of Asaph.

¹Truly God is good to Israel,
     to those whose hearts are pure.

²But as for me, I came so close to the edge of the cliff!
     My feet were slipping, and I was almost gone.

³For I envied the proud
   when I saw them prosper despite their wickedness.
⁴They seem to live such a painless life;
   their bodies are so healthy and strong.
⁵They aren't troubled like other people
   or plagued with problems like everyone else.
⁶They wear pride like a jeweled necklace,
   and their clothing is woven of cruelty.
⁷These fat cats have everything
   their hearts could ever wish for!
⁸They scoff and speak only evil;
   in their pride they seek to crush others.
⁹They boast against the very heavens,
   and their words strut throughout the earth.
¹⁰And so the people are dismayed and confused,
   drinking in all their words.
¹¹"Does God realize what is going on?" they ask.
   "Is the Most High even aware of what is happening?"
¹²Look at these arrogant people—
   enjoying a life of ease while their riches multiply.

¹³Was it for nothing that I kept my heart pure
   and kept myself from doing wrong?
¹⁴All I get is trouble all day long;
   every morning brings me pain.

¹⁵If I had really spoken this way,
    I would have been a traitor to your people.
¹⁶So I tried to understand why the wicked prosper.
    But what a difficult task it is!
¹⁷Then one day I went into your sanctuary, O God,
    and I thought about the destiny of the wicked.
¹⁸Truly, you put them on a slippery path
    and send them sliding over the cliff to destruction.
¹⁹In an instant they are destroyed,
    swept away by terrors.
²⁰Their present life is only a dream
    that is gone when they awake.
When you arise, O Lord,
    you will make them vanish from this life.

²¹Then I realized how bitter I had become,
    how pained I had been by all I had seen.
²²I was so foolish and ignorant—
    I must have seemed like a senseless animal to you.
²³Yet I still belong to you;
    you are holding my right hand.
²⁴You will keep on guiding me with your counsel,
    leading me to a glorious destiny.
²⁵Whom have I in heaven but you?
    I desire you more than anything on earth.

²⁶My health may fail, and my spirit may grow weak,

but God remains the strength of my heart;

he is mine forever.

²⁷But those who desert him will perish,

for you destroy those who abandon you.

²⁸But as for me, how good it is to be near God!

I have made the Sovereign LORD my shelter,

and I will tell everyone about the wonderful things
you do.

PSALM 74

A psalm of Asaph.

¹O God, why have you rejected us forever?

Why is your anger so intense against the sheep of your
own pasture?

²Remember that we are the people you chose in ancient
times,

the tribe you redeemed as your own special possession!

And remember Jerusalem, your home here on earth.

³Walk through the awful ruins of the city;

see how the enemy has destroyed your sanctuary.

⁴There your enemies shouted their victorious battle cries;

there they set up their battle standards.

⁵They chopped down the entrance
    like woodcutters in a forest.
⁶With axes and picks,
    they smashed the carved paneling.
⁷They set the sanctuary on fire, burning it to the ground.
    They utterly defiled the place that bears your holy
        name.
⁸Then they thought, "Let's destroy everything!"
    So they burned down all the places where God was
        worshiped.

⁹We see no miraculous signs
    as evidence that you will save us.
All the prophets are gone;
    no one can tell us when it will end.
¹⁰How long, O God, will you allow our enemies to mock
        you?
    Will you let them dishonor your name forever?
¹¹Why do you hold back your strong right hand?
    Unleash your powerful fist and deliver a deathblow.

¹²You, O God, are my king from ages past,
    bringing salvation to the earth.
¹³You split the sea by your strength
    and smashed the sea monster's heads.

¹⁴You crushed the heads of Leviathan
   and let the desert animals eat him.
¹⁵You caused the springs and streams to gush forth,
   and you dried up rivers that never run dry.
¹⁶Both day and night belong to you;
   you made the starlight and the sun.
¹⁷You set the boundaries of the earth,
   and you make both summer and winter.

¹⁸See how these enemies scoff at you, LORD.
   A foolish nation has dishonored your name.
¹⁹Don't let these wild beasts destroy your doves.
   Don't forget your afflicted people forever.

²⁰Remember your covenant promises,
   for the land is full of darkness and violence!
²¹Don't let the downtrodden be constantly disgraced!
   Instead, let these poor and needy ones give praise to
      your name.

²²Arise, O God, and defend your cause.
   Remember how these fools insult you all day long.
²³Don't overlook these things your enemies have said.
   Their uproar of rebellion grows ever louder.

PSALM 75

For the choir director: A psalm of Asaph, to be sung to the tune "Do Not Destroy!" A song.

¹We thank you, O God!
    We give thanks because you are near.
    People everywhere tell of your mighty miracles.

²God says, "At the time I have planned,
    I will bring justice against the wicked.
³When the earth quakes and its people live in turmoil,
    I am the one who keeps its foundations firm.   *Interlude*

⁴"I warned the proud, 'Stop your boasting!'
    I told the wicked, 'Don't raise your fists!
⁵Don't lift your fists in defiance at the heavens
    or speak with rebellious arrogance.' "

⁶For no one on earth—from east or west,
    or even from the wilderness—
    can raise another person up.
⁷It is God alone who judges;
    he decides who will rise and who will fall.
⁸For the LORD holds a cup in his hand;
    it is full of foaming wine mixed with spices.

He pours the wine out in judgment,
    and all the wicked must drink it,
        draining it to the dregs.

⁹But as for me, I will always proclaim what God has done;
    I will sing praises to the God of Israel.

¹⁰For God says, "I will cut off the strength of the wicked,
    but I will increase the power of the godly."

PROVERBS 15

A gentle answer turns away wrath, but harsh words stir up
anger.

²The wise person makes learning a joy; fools spout
only foolishness.

³The LORD is watching everywhere, keeping his eye
on both the evil and the good.

⁴Gentle words bring life and health; a deceitful tongue
crushes the spirit.

⁵Only a fool despises a parent's discipline; whoever
learns from correction is wise.

⁶There is treasure in the house of the godly, but the
earnings of the wicked bring trouble.

⁷Only the wise can give good advice; fools cannot
do so.

⁸The LORD hates the sacrifice of the wicked, but he delights in the prayers of the upright.

⁹The LORD despises the way of the wicked, but he loves those who pursue godliness.

¹⁰Whoever abandons the right path will be severely punished; whoever hates correction will die.

¹¹Even the depths of Death and Destruction are known by the LORD. How much more does he know the human heart!

¹²Mockers don't love those who rebuke them, so they stay away from the wise.

¹³A glad heart makes a happy face; a broken heart crushes the spirit.

¹⁴A wise person is hungry for truth, while the fool feeds on trash.

¹⁵For the poor, every day brings trouble; for the happy heart, life is a continual feast.

¹⁶It is better to have little with fear for the LORD than to have great treasure with turmoil.

¹⁷A bowl of soup with someone you love is better than steak with someone you hate.

¹⁸A hothead starts fights; a cool-tempered person tries to stop them.

¹⁹A lazy person has trouble all through life; the path of the upright is easy!

²⁰Sensible children bring joy to their father; foolish children despise their mother.

²¹Foolishness brings joy to those who have no sense; a sensible person stays on the right path.

²²Plans go wrong for lack of advice; many counselors bring success.

²³Everyone enjoys a fitting reply; it is wonderful to say the right thing at the right time!

²⁴The path of the wise leads to life above; they leave the grave behind.

²⁵The LORD destroys the house of the proud, but he protects the property of widows.

²⁶The LORD despises the thoughts of the wicked, but he delights in pure words.

²⁷Dishonest money brings grief to the whole family, but those who hate bribes will live.

²⁸The godly think before speaking; the wicked spout evil words.

²⁹The LORD is far from the wicked, but he hears the prayers of the righteous.

³⁰A cheerful look brings joy to the heart; good news makes for good health.

³¹If you listen to constructive criticism, you will be at home among the wise.

³²If you reject criticism, you only harm yourself; but if you listen to correction, you grow in understanding.

³³Fear of the LORD teaches a person to be wise; humility precedes honor.

DAY SIXTEEN

PSALM 76

For the choir director: A psalm of Asaph, to be accompanied by stringed instruments. A song.

¹God is well known in Judah;
   his name is great in Israel.
²Jerusalem is where he lives;
   Mount Zion is his home.
³There he breaks the arrows of the enemy,
   the shields and swords and weapons of his foes.   *Interlude*

⁴You are glorious and more majestic
   than the everlasting mountains.
⁵The mightiest of our enemies have been plundered.
   They lie before us in the sleep of death.
   No warrior could lift a hand against us.
⁶When you rebuked them, O God of Jacob,
   their horses and chariots stood still.

⁷No wonder you are greatly feared!
   Who can stand before you when your anger explodes?

⁸From heaven you sentenced your enemies;
the earth trembled and stood silent before you.
⁹You stand up to judge those who do evil, O God,
and to rescue the oppressed of the earth.   *Interlude*

¹⁰Human opposition only enhances your glory,
for you use it as a sword of judgment.

¹¹Make vows to the LORD your God, and fulfill them.
Let everyone bring tribute to the Awesome One.
¹²For he breaks the spirit of princes
and is feared by the kings of the earth.

PSALM 77

For Jeduthun, the choir director: A psalm of Asaph.

¹I cry out to God without holding back.
Oh, that God would listen to me!
²When I was in deep trouble,
I searched for the Lord.
All night long I pray, with hands lifted toward heaven,
pleading.
There can be no joy for me until he acts.
³I think of God, and I moan,
overwhelmed with longing for his help.   *Interlude*

⁴You don't let me sleep.

I am too distressed even to pray!

⁵I think of the good old days, long since ended,

⁶   when my nights were filled with joyful songs.

I search my soul and think about the difference now.

⁷Has the Lord rejected me forever?

Will he never again show me favor?

⁸Is his unfailing love gone forever?

Have his promises permanently failed?

⁹Has God forgotten to be kind?

Has he slammed the door on his compassion? *Interlude*

¹⁰And I said, "This is my fate,

that the blessings of the Most High have changed to
hatred."

¹¹I recall all you have done, O LORD;

I remember your wonderful deeds of long ago.

¹²They are constantly in my thoughts.

I cannot stop thinking about them.

¹³O God, your ways are holy.

Is there any god as mighty as you?

¹⁴You are the God of miracles and wonders!

You demonstrate your awesome power among the
nations.

¹⁵You have redeemed your people by your strength,
　　the descendants of Jacob and of Joseph by your might.

Interlude

¹⁶When the Red Sea saw you, O God,
　　its waters looked and trembled!
　　The sea quaked to its very depths.
¹⁷The clouds poured down their rain;
　　the thunder rolled and crackled in the sky.
　　Your arrows of lightning flashed.
¹⁸Your thunder roared from the whirlwind;
　　the lightning lit up the world!
　　The earth trembled and shook.
¹⁹Your road led through the sea,
　　your pathway through the mighty waters—
　　a pathway no one knew was there!
²⁰You led your people along that road like a flock of sheep,
　　with Moses and Aaron as their shepherds.

PSALM 78

A psalm of Asaph.

¹O my people, listen to my teaching.
　　Open your ears to what I am saying,
² 　　for I will speak to you in a parable.

I will teach you hidden lessons from our past—

³ stories we have heard and know,
   stories our ancestors handed down to us.
⁴We will not hide these truths from our children
   but will tell the next generation about the glorious
      deeds of the LORD.
   We will tell of his power and the mighty miracles he
      did.
⁵For he issued his decree to Jacob;
   he gave his law to Israel.
He commanded our ancestors
   to teach them to their children,
⁶so the next generation might know them—
   even the children not yet born—
   that they in turn might teach their children.
⁷So each generation can set its hope anew on God,
   remembering his glorious miracles
   and obeying his commands.
⁸Then they will not be like their ancestors—
   stubborn, rebellious, and unfaithful,
   refusing to give their hearts to God.

⁹The warriors of Ephraim, though fully armed,
   turned their backs and fled when the day of battle
      came.

¹⁰They did not keep God's covenant,
　　and they refused to live by his law.
¹¹They forgot what he had done—
　　the wonderful miracles he had shown them,
¹²　　the miracles he did for their ancestors in Egypt, on the
　　　　plain of Zoan.
¹³For he divided the sea before them and led them
　　　　through!
　　The water stood up like walls beside them!
¹⁴In the daytime he led them by a cloud,
　　and at night by a pillar of fire.
¹⁵He split open the rocks in the wilderness
　　to give them plenty of water, as from a gushing
　　　　spring.
¹⁶He made streams pour from the rock,
　　making the waters flow down like a river!

¹⁷Yet they kept on with their sin,
　　rebelling against the Most High in the desert.
¹⁸They willfully tested God in their hearts,
　　demanding the foods they craved.
¹⁹They even spoke against God himself, saying,
　　"God can't give us food in the desert.
²⁰Yes, he can strike a rock so water gushes out,
　　but he can't give his people bread and meat."

²¹When the LORD heard them, he was angry.

The fire of his wrath burned against Jacob.

Yes, his anger rose against Israel,

²²   for they did not believe God

or trust him to care for them.

²³But he commanded the skies to open—

he opened the doors of heaven—

²⁴   and rained down manna for them to eat.

He gave them bread from heaven.

²⁵   They ate the food of angels!

God gave them all they could hold.

²⁶He released the east wind in the heavens

and guided the south wind by his mighty power.

²⁷He rained down meat as thick as dust—

birds as plentiful as the sands along the seashore!

²⁸He caused the birds to fall within their camp

and all around their tents.

²⁹The people ate their fill.

He gave them what they wanted.

³⁰But before they finished eating this food they had craved,

while the meat was yet in their mouths,

³¹the anger of God rose against them,

and he killed their strongest men;

he struck down the finest of Israel's young men.

³²But in spite of this, the people kept on sinning.

    They refused to believe in his miracles.

³³So he ended their lives in failure

    and gave them years of terror.

³⁴When God killed some of them, the rest finally

       sought him.

    They repented and turned to God.

³⁵Then they remembered that God was their rock,

    that their redeemer was the Most High.

³⁶But they followed him only with their words;

    they lied to him with their tongues.

³⁷Their hearts were not loyal to him.

    They did not keep his covenant.

³⁸Yet he was merciful and forgave their sins

    and didn't destroy them all.

Many a time he held back his anger

    and did not unleash his fury!

³⁹For he remembered that they were merely mortal,

    gone in a moment like a breath of wind, never to return.

⁴⁰Oh, how often they rebelled against him in the desert

    and grieved his heart in the wilderness.

⁴¹Again and again they tested God's patience

    and frustrated the Holy One of Israel.

⁴²They forgot about his power
and how he rescued them from their enemies.
⁴³They forgot his miraculous signs in Egypt,
his wonders on the plain of Zoan.
⁴⁴For he turned their rivers into blood,
so no one could drink from the streams.
⁴⁵He sent vast swarms of flies to consume them
and hordes of frogs to ruin them.
⁴⁶He gave their crops to caterpillars;
their harvest was consumed by locusts.
⁴⁷He destroyed their grapevines with hail
and shattered their sycamores with sleet.
⁴⁸He abandoned their cattle to the hail,
their livestock to bolts of lightning.
⁴⁹He loosed on them his fierce anger—
all his fury, rage, and hostility.
He dispatched against them
a band of destroying angels.
⁵⁰He turned his anger against them;
he did not spare the Egyptians' lives
but handed them over to the plague.
⁵¹He killed the oldest son in each Egyptian family,
the flower of youth throughout the land of Egypt.

⁵²But he led his own people like a flock of sheep,
   guiding them safely through the wilderness.
⁵³He kept them safe so they were not afraid;
   but the sea closed in upon their enemies.
⁵⁴He brought them to the border of his holy land,
   to this land of hills he had won for them.
⁵⁵He drove out the nations before them;
   he gave them their inheritance by lot.
   He settled the tribes of Israel into their homes.

⁵⁶Yet though he did all this for them,
   they continued to test his patience.
They rebelled against the Most High
   and refused to follow his decrees.
⁵⁷They turned back and were as faithless as their parents
         had been.
   They were as useless as a crooked bow.
⁵⁸They made God angry by building altars to other gods;
   they made him jealous with their idols.
⁵⁹When God heard them, he was very angry,
   and he rejected Israel completely.
⁶⁰Then he abandoned his dwelling at Shiloh,
   the Tabernacle where he had lived among the people.
⁶¹He allowed the Ark of his might to be captured;
   he surrendered his glory into enemy hands.

⁶²He gave his people over to be butchered by the sword,
  because he was so angry with his own people—his
    special possession.
⁶³Their young men were killed by fire;
  their young women died before singing their wedding
    songs.
⁶⁴Their priests were slaughtered,
  and their widows could not mourn their deaths.
⁶⁵Then the Lord rose up as though waking from sleep,
  like a mighty man aroused from a drunken stupor.
⁶⁶He routed his enemies
  and sent them to eternal shame.
⁶⁷But he rejected Joseph's descendants;
  he did not choose the tribe of Ephraim.
⁶⁸He chose instead the tribe of Judah,
  Mount Zion, which he loved.
⁶⁹There he built his towering sanctuary,
  as solid and enduring as the earth itself.
⁷⁰He chose his servant David,
  calling him from the sheep pens.
⁷¹He took David from tending the ewes and lambs
  and made him the shepherd of Jacob's
    descendants—
      God's own people, Israel.

^{72}He cared for them with a true heart
and led them with skillful hands.

PSALM 79

A psalm of Asaph.

^{1}O God, pagan nations have conquered your land, your
special possession.
They have defiled your holy Temple
and made Jerusalem a heap of ruins.
^{2}They have left the bodies of your servants
as food for the birds of heaven.
The flesh of your godly ones
has become food for the wild animals.
^{3}Blood has flowed like water all around Jerusalem;
no one is left to bury the dead.
^{4}We are mocked by our neighbors,
an object of scorn and derision to those around us.

^{5}O LORD, how long will you be angry with us?
Forever?
How long will your jealousy burn like fire?
^{6}Pour out your wrath on the nations that refuse to
recognize you—
on kingdoms that do not call upon your name.

⁷For they have devoured your people Israel,
     making the land a desolate wilderness.
⁸Oh, do not hold us guilty for our former sins!
          Let your tenderhearted mercies quickly meet our
               needs,
          for we are brought low to the dust.
⁹Help us, O God of our salvation!
     Help us for the honor of your name.
Oh, save us and forgive our sins
     for the sake of your name.
¹⁰Why should pagan nations be allowed to scoff,
     asking, "Where is their God?"
Show us your vengeance against the nations,
     for they have spilled the blood of your servants.
¹¹Listen to the moaning of the prisoners.
     Demonstrate your great power by saving those
          condemned to die.

¹²O Lord, take sevenfold vengeance on our neighbors
     for the scorn they have hurled at you.
¹³Then we your people, the sheep of your pasture,
     will thank you forever and ever,
          praising your greatness from generation to
               generation.

We can gather our thoughts, but the LORD gives the right answer.

²People may be pure in their own eyes, but the LORD examines their motives.

³Commit your work to the LORD, and then your plans will succeed.

⁴The LORD has made everything for his own purposes, even the wicked for punishment.

⁵The LORD despises pride; be assured that the proud will be punished.

⁶Unfailing love and faithfulness cover sin; evil is avoided by fear of the LORD.

⁷When the ways of people please the LORD, he makes even their enemies live at peace with them.

⁸It is better to be poor and godly than rich and dishonest.

⁹We can make our plans, but the LORD determines our steps.

¹⁰The king speaks with divine wisdom; he must never judge unfairly.

¹¹The LORD demands fairness in every business deal; he sets the standard.

¹²A king despises wrongdoing, for his rule depends on his justice.

¹³The king is pleased with righteous lips; he loves those who speak honestly.

¹⁴The anger of the king is a deadly threat; the wise do what they can to appease it.

¹⁵When the king smiles, there is life; his favor refreshes like a gentle rain.

¹⁶How much better to get wisdom than gold, and understanding than silver!

¹⁷The path of the upright leads away from evil; whoever follows that path is safe.

¹⁸Pride goes before destruction, and haughtiness before a fall.

¹⁹It is better to live humbly with the poor than to share plunder with the proud.

²⁰Those who listen to instruction will prosper; those who trust the LORD will be happy.

²¹The wise are known for their understanding, and instruction is appreciated if it's well presented.

²²Discretion is a life-giving fountain to those who possess it, but discipline is wasted on fools.

²³From a wise mind comes wise speech; the words of the wise are persuasive.

²⁴Kind words are like honey—sweet to the soul and healthy for the body.

²⁵There is a path before each person that seems right, but it ends in death.

²⁶It is good for workers to have an appetite; an empty stomach drives them on.

²⁷Scoundrels hunt for scandal; their words are a destructive blaze.

²⁸A troublemaker plants seeds of strife; gossip separates the best of friends.

²⁹Violent people deceive their companions, leading them down a harmful path.

³⁰With narrowed eyes, they plot evil; without a word, they plan their mischief.

³¹Gray hair is a crown of glory; it is gained by living a godly life.

³²It is better to be patient than powerful; it is better to have self-control than to conquer a city.

³³We may throw the dice, but the LORD determines how they fall.

PSALM 80

For the choir director: A psalm of Asaph, to be sung to the tune "Lilies of the Covenant."

¹Please listen, O Shepherd of Israel,
>   you who lead Israel like a flock.
O God, enthroned above the cherubim,
>   display your radiant glory
2   to Ephraim, Benjamin, and Manasseh.
Show us your mighty power.
>   Come to rescue us!

³Turn us again to yourself, O God.
>   Make your face shine down upon us.
>   Only then will we be saved.

⁴O Lord God Almighty,
>   how long will you be angry and reject our prayers?
⁵You have fed us with sorrow
>   and made us drink tears by the bucketful.

⁶You have made us the scorn of neighboring nations.
>   Our enemies treat us as a joke.

⁷Turn us again to yourself, O God Almighty.
>   Make your face shine down upon us.
>   Only then will we be saved.
⁸You brought us from Egypt as though we were a tender
>   vine;
>   you drove away the pagan nations and transplanted us
>   into your land.
⁹You cleared the ground for us,
>   and we took root and filled the land.
¹⁰The mountains were covered with our shade;
>   the mighty cedars were covered with our branches.
¹¹We spread our branches west to the Mediterranean Sea,
>   our limbs east to the Euphrates River.
¹²But now, why have you broken down our walls
>   so that all who pass may steal our fruit?
¹³The boar from the forest devours us,
>   and the wild animals feed on us.

¹⁴Come back, we beg you, O God Almighty.
>   Look down from heaven and see our plight.
Watch over and care for this vine
¹⁵   that you yourself have planted,
>   this son you have raised for yourself.

¹⁶For we are chopped up and burned by our enemies.

    May they perish at the sight of your frown.

¹⁷Strengthen the man you love,

    the son of your choice.

¹⁸Then we will never forsake you again.

    Revive us so we can call on your name once more.

¹⁹Turn us again to yourself, O Lord God Almighty.

    Make your face shine down upon us.

    Only then will we be saved.

PSALM 81

For the choir director: A psalm of Asaph, to be accompanied by a stringed instrument.

¹Sing praises to God, our strength.

    Sing to the God of Israel.

²Sing! Beat the tambourine.

    Play the sweet lyre and the harp.

³Sound the trumpet for a sacred feast

    when the moon is new,

    when the moon is full.

⁴For this is required by the laws of Israel;

    it is a law of the God of Jacob.

⁵He made it a decree for Israel
      when he attacked Egypt to set us free.

I heard an unknown voice that said,
  ⁶"Now I will relieve your shoulder of its burden;
      I will free your hands from their heavy tasks.
⁷You cried to me in trouble, and I saved you;
      I answered out of the thundercloud.
I tested your faith at Meribah,
      when you complained that there was no water *Interlude*

⁸"Listen to me, O my people, while I give you stern
            warnings.
      O Israel, if you would only listen!
⁹You must never have a foreign god;
      you must not bow down before a false god.
¹⁰For it was I, the LORD your God,
      who rescued you from the land of Egypt.
      Open your mouth wide, and I will fill it with good things.

¹¹"But no, my people wouldn't listen.
      Israel did not want me around.
¹²So I let them follow their blind and stubborn way,
      living according to their own desires.
¹³But oh, that my people would listen to me!
      Oh, that Israel would follow me, walking in my paths!

¹⁴How quickly I would then subdue their enemies!

How soon my hands would be upon their foes!
¹⁵Those who hate the LORD would cringe before him;

their desolation would last forever.
¹⁶But I would feed you with the best of foods.

I would satisfy you with wild honey from the rock."

PSALM 82

A psalm of Asaph.

¹God presides over heaven's court;

he pronounces judgment on the judges:
²"How long will you judges hand down unjust
decisions?

How long will you shower special favors on the
wicked? *Interlude*

³"Give fair judgment to the poor and the orphan;

uphold the rights of the oppressed and the destitute.
⁴Rescue the poor and helpless;

deliver them from the grasp of evil people.
⁵But these oppressors know nothing;

they are so ignorant!
And because they are in darkness,

the whole world is shaken to the core.

⁶I say, 'You are gods
and children of the Most High.
⁷But in death you are mere men.
You will fall as any prince,
for all must die.' "

⁸Rise up, O God, and judge the earth,
for all the nations belong to you.

PSALM 83

A psalm of Asaph. A song.

¹O God, don't sit idly by,
silent and inactive!
²Don't you hear the tumult of your enemies?
Don't you see what your arrogant enemies are
doing?
³They devise crafty schemes against your people,
laying plans against your precious ones.
⁴"Come," they say, "let us wipe out Israel as a nation.
We will destroy the very memory of its existence."
⁵   This was their unanimous decision.
They signed a treaty as allies against you—
⁶   these Edomites and Ishmaelites,
Moabites and Hagrites,

7 Gebalites, Ammonites, and Amalekites,
      and people from Philistia and Tyre.
8Assyria has joined them, too,
      and is allied with the descendants of Lot.   *Interlude*

9Do to them as you did to the Midianites
      or as you did to Sisera and Jabin at the Kishon River.
10They were destroyed at Endor,
      and their decaying corpses fertilized the soil.
11Let their mighty nobles die as Oreb and Zeeb did.
      Let all their princes die like Zebah and Zalmunna,
12for they said, "Let us seize for our own use
      these pasturelands of God!"

13O my God, blow them away like whirling dust,
      like chaff before the wind!
14As a fire roars through a forest
      and as a flame sets mountains ablaze,
15chase them with your fierce storms;
      terrify them with your tempests.
16Utterly disgrace them
      until they submit to your name, O Lord.
17Let them be ashamed and terrified forever.
      Make them failures in everything they do,
18until they learn that you alone are called the Lord,

that you alone are the Most High, supreme over all
the earth.

PSALM 84

*For the choir director: A psalm of the descendants of Korah, to be
accompanied by a stringed instrument.*

¹How lovely is your dwelling place,
    O LORD Almighty.
²I long, yes, I faint with longing
    to enter the courts of the LORD.
With my whole being, body and soul,
    I will shout joyfully to the living God.
³Even the sparrow finds a home there,
    and the swallow builds her nest
    and raises her young—
    at a place near your altar,
    O LORD Almighty, my King and my God!
⁴How happy are those who can live in your house,
    always singing your praises.   *Interlude*

⁵Happy are those who are strong in the LORD,
    who set their minds on a pilgrimage to Jerusalem.
⁶When they walk through the Valley of Weeping,
    it will become a place of refreshing springs,
    where pools of blessing collect after the rains!

⁷They will continue to grow stronger,
    and each of them will appear before God in Jerusalem.

⁸O L ORD God Almighty, hear my prayer.
    Listen, O God of Israel.   *Interlude*

⁹O God, look with favor upon the king, our protector!
    Have mercy on the one you have anointed.

¹⁰A single day in your courts
    is better than a thousand anywhere else!
I would rather be a gatekeeper in the house of my God
    than live the good life in the homes of the wicked.
¹¹For the L ORD God is our light and protector.
    He gives us grace and glory.
No good thing will the L ORD withhold
    from those who do what is right.
¹²O L ORD Almighty,
    happy are those who trust in you.

PSALM 85

For the choir director: A psalm of the descendants of Korah.

¹L ORD, you have poured out amazing blessings on your
    land!
    You have restored the fortunes of Israel.

²You have forgiven the guilt of your people—
    yes, you have covered all their sins.   *Interlude*

³You have withdrawn your fury.
    You have ended your blazing anger.
⁴Now turn to us again, O God of our salvation.
    Put aside your anger against us.
⁵Will you be angry with us always?
    Will you prolong your wrath to distant generations?
⁶Won't you revive us again,
    so your people can rejoice in you?
⁷Show us your unfailing love, O LORD,
    and grant us your salvation.

⁸I listen carefully to what God the LORD is saying,
    for he speaks peace to his people, his faithful ones.
    But let them not return to their foolish ways.
⁹Surely his salvation is near to those who honor him;
    our land will be filled with his glory.

¹⁰Unfailing love and truth have met together.
    Righteousness and peace have kissed!
¹¹Truth springs up from the earth,
    and righteousness smiles down from heaven.
¹²Yes, the LORD pours down his blessings.
    Our land will yield its bountiful crops.

¹³Righteousness goes as a herald before him,
    preparing the way for his steps.

PROVERBS 17

A dry crust eaten in peace is better than a great feast with strife.

²A wise slave will rule over the master's shameful sons and will share their inheritance.

³Fire tests the purity of silver and gold, but the LORD tests the heart.

⁴Wrongdoers listen to wicked talk; liars pay attention to destructive words.

⁵Those who mock the poor insult their Maker; those who rejoice at the misfortune of others will be punished.

⁶Grandchildren are the crowning glory of the aged; parents are the pride of their children.

⁷Eloquent speech is not fitting for a fool; even less are lies fitting for a ruler.

⁸A bribe seems to work like magic for those who give it; they succeed in all they do.

⁹Disregarding another person's faults preserves love; telling about them separates close friends.

¹⁰A single rebuke does more for a person of understanding than a hundred lashes on the back of a fool.

¹¹Evil people seek rebellion, but they will be severely punished.

¹²It is safer to meet a bear robbed of her cubs than to confront a fool caught in folly.

¹³If you repay evil for good, evil will never leave your house.

¹⁴Beginning a quarrel is like opening a floodgate, so drop the matter before a dispute breaks out.

¹⁵The LORD despises those who acquit the guilty and condemn the innocent.

¹⁶It is senseless to pay tuition to educate a fool who has no heart for wisdom.

¹⁷A friend is always loyal, and a brother is born to help in time of need.

¹⁸It is poor judgment to co-sign a friend's note, to become responsible for a neighbor's debts.

¹⁹Anyone who loves to quarrel loves sin; anyone who speaks boastfully invites disaster.

²⁰The crooked heart will not prosper; the twisted tongue tumbles into trouble.

²¹It is painful to be the parent of a fool; there is no joy for the father of a rebel.

²²A cheerful heart is good medicine, but a broken spirit saps a person's strength.

²³The wicked accept secret bribes to pervert justice.

²⁴Sensible people keep their eyes glued on wisdom, but a fool's eyes wander to the ends of the earth.

²⁵A foolish child brings grief to a father and bitterness to a mother.

²⁶It is wrong to fine the godly for being good or to punish nobles for being honest!

²⁷A truly wise person uses few words; a person with understanding is even-tempered.

²⁸Even fools are thought to be wise when they keep silent; when they keep their mouths shut, they seem intelligent.

DAY EIGHTEEN

PSALM 86

A prayer of David.

¹Bend down, O LORD, and hear my prayer;
    answer me, for I need your help.
²Protect me, for I am devoted to you.
    Save me, for I serve you and trust you.
    You are my God.
³Be merciful, O Lord,
    for I am calling on you constantly.
⁴Give me happiness, O Lord,
    for my life depends on you.
⁵O Lord, you are so good, so ready to forgive,
    so full of unfailing love for all who ask your aid.
⁶Listen closely to my prayer, O LORD;
    hear my urgent cry.
⁷I will call to you whenever trouble strikes,
    and you will answer me.

8Nowhere among the pagan gods is there a god like you,
    O Lord.
    There are no other miracles like yours.
9All the nations—and you made each one—
    will come and bow before you, Lord;
    they will praise your great and holy name.
10For you are great and perform great miracles.
    You alone are God.

11Teach me your ways, O LORD,
    that I may live according to your truth!
Grant me purity of heart,
    that I may honor you.
12With all my heart I will praise you, O Lord my God.
    I will give glory to your name forever,
13for your love for me is very great.
    You have rescued me from the depths of death!

14O God, insolent people rise up against me;
    violent people are trying to kill me.
    And you mean nothing to them.
15But you, O Lord, are a merciful and gracious God,
    slow to get angry,
    full of unfailing love and truth.
16Look down and have mercy on me.

Give strength to your servant;

yes, save me, for I am your servant.

¹⁷Send me a sign of your favor.

Then those who hate me will be put to shame,

for you, O LORD, help and comfort me.

PSALM 87

A psalm of the descendants of Korah. A song.

¹On the holy mountain stands the city founded by the
LORD.

²   He loves the city of Jerusalem

more than any other city in Israel.

³O city of God,

what glorious things are said of you!   *Interlude*

⁴I will record Egypt and Babylon among those who know
me—

also Philistia and Tyre, and even distant Ethiopia.

They have all become citizens of Jerusalem!

⁵And it will be said of Jerusalem,

"Everyone has become a citizen here."

And the Most High will personally bless this city.

⁶When the LORD registers the nations,

he will say, "This one has become a citizen of
　　Jerusalem."   *Interlude*

⁷At all the festivals, the people will sing,
　　"The source of my life is in Jerusalem!"

PSALM 88

For the choir director: A psalm of the descendants of Korah, to be sung
to the tune "The Suffering of Affliction." A psalm of Heman the
Ezrahite. A song.

¹O LORD, God of my salvation,
　　I have cried out to you day and night.
²Now hear my prayer;
　　listen to my cry.
³For my life is full of troubles,
　　and death draws near.
⁴I have been dismissed as one who is dead,
　　like a strong man with no strength left.
⁵They have abandoned me to death,
　　and I am as good as dead.
I am forgotten,
　　cut off from your care.
⁶You have thrust me down to the lowest pit,
　　into the darkest depths.

⁷Your anger lies heavy on me;
    wave after wave engulfs me.   *Interlude*

⁸You have caused my friends to loathe me;
    you have sent them all away.
I am in a trap with no way of escape.
  ⁹ My eyes are blinded by my tears.
Each day I beg for your help, O LORD;
    I lift my pleading hands to you for mercy.
¹⁰Of what use to the dead are your miracles?
    Do the dead get up and praise you?   *Interlude*

¹¹Can those in the grave declare your unfailing love?
    In the place of destruction, can they proclaim your
        faithfulness?
¹²Can the darkness speak of your miracles?
    Can anyone in the land of forgetfulness talk about
        your righteousness?

¹³O LORD, I cry out to you.
    I will keep on pleading day by day.
¹⁴O LORD, why do you reject me?
    Why do you turn your face away from me?
¹⁵I have been sickly and close to death since my youth.
    I stand helpless and desperate before your terrors.

¹⁶Your fierce anger has overwhelmed me.
Your terrors have cut me off.
¹⁷They swirl around me like floodwaters all day long.
They have encircled me completely.
¹⁸You have taken away my companions and loved ones;
only darkness remains.

PSALM 89

A psalm of Ethan the Ezrahite.

¹I will sing of the tender mercies of the LORD forever!
Young and old will hear of your faithfulness.
²Your unfailing love will last forever.
Your faithfulness is as enduring as the heavens.

³The LORD said, "I have made a solemn agreement with
David, my chosen servant.
I have sworn this oath to him:
⁴'I will establish your descendants as kings forever;
they will sit on your throne from now until
eternity.' "   *Interlude*

⁵All heaven will praise your miracles, LORD;
myriads of angels will praise you for your
faithfulness.

⁶For who in all of heaven can compare with the LORD?

What mightiest angel is anything like the LORD?

⁷The highest angelic powers stand in awe of God.

He is far more awesome than those who surround his
throne.

⁸O LORD God Almighty!

Where is there anyone as mighty as you, LORD?

Faithfulness is your very character.

⁹You are the one who rules the oceans.

When their waves rise in fearful storms, you subdue
them.

¹⁰You are the one who crushed the great sea monster.

You scattered your enemies with your mighty arm.

¹¹The heavens are yours, and the earth is yours;

everything in the world is yours—you created it all.

¹²You created north and south.

Mount Tabor and Mount Hermon praise your name.

¹³Powerful is your arm!

Strong is your hand!

Your right hand is lifted high in glorious strength.

¹⁴Your throne is founded on two strong pillars—

righteousness and justice.

Unfailing love and truth walk before you as
attendants.

¹⁵Happy are those who hear the joyful call to worship,
>   for they will walk in the light of your presence, LORD.
¹⁶They rejoice all day long in your wonderful reputation.
>   They exult in your righteousness.
¹⁷You are their glorious strength.
>   Our power is based on your favor.
¹⁸Yes, our protection comes from the LORD,
>   and he, the Holy One of Israel, has given us our king.

¹⁹You once spoke in a vision to your prophet and said,
>   "I have given help to a warrior.
>   I have selected him from the common people to be king.
²⁰I have found my servant David.
>   I have anointed him with my holy oil.
²¹I will steady him,
>   and I will make him strong.
²²His enemies will not get the best of him,
>   nor will the wicked overpower him.
²³I will beat down his adversaries before him
>   and destroy those who hate him.
²⁴My faithfulness and unfailing love will be with him,
>   and he will rise to power because of me.
²⁵I will extend his rule from the Mediterranean Sea in the
>   west
>   to the Tigris and Euphrates rivers in the east.

²⁶And he will say to me, 'You are my Father,
        my God, and the Rock of my salvation.'
²⁷I will make him my firstborn son,
        the mightiest king on earth.
²⁸I will love him and be kind to him forever;
        my covenant with him will never end.
²⁹I will preserve an heir for him;
        his throne will be as endless as the days of heaven.
³⁰But if his sons forsake my law
        and fail to walk in my ways,
³¹if they do not obey my decrees
        and fail to keep my commands,
³²then I will punish their sin with the rod,
        and their disobedience with beating.
³³But I will never stop loving him,
        nor let my promise to him fail.
³⁴No, I will not break my covenant;
        I will not take back a single word I said.
³⁵I have sworn an oath to David,
        and in my holiness I cannot lie:
³⁶His dynasty will go on forever;
        his throne is as secure as the sun,
³⁷   as eternal as the moon,
        my faithful witness in the sky!"   *Interlude*

³⁸But now you have rejected him.

Why are you so angry with the one you chose as king?
³⁹You have renounced your covenant with him,

for you have thrown his crown in the dust.
⁴⁰You have broken down the walls protecting him

and laid in ruins every fort defending him.
⁴¹Everyone who comes along has robbed him

while his neighbors mock.
⁴²You have strengthened his enemies against him

and made them all rejoice.
⁴³You have made his sword useless

and have refused to help him in battle.
⁴⁴You have ended his splendor

and overturned his throne.
⁴⁵You have made him old before his time

and publicly disgraced him.   *Interlude*

⁴⁶O Lᴏʀᴅ, how long will this go on?

Will you hide yourself forever?

How long will your anger burn like fire?
⁴⁷Remember how short my life is,

how empty and futile this human existence!
⁴⁸No one can live forever; all will die.

No one can escape the power of the grave.   *Interlude*

⁴⁹Lord, where is your unfailing love?
>   You promised it to David with a faithful pledge.
⁵⁰Consider, Lord, how your servants are disgraced!
>   I carry in my heart the insults of so many people.
⁵¹Your enemies have mocked me, O LORD;
>   they mock the one you anointed as king.

⁵²Blessed be the LORD forever!
>   Amen and amen!

BOOK FOUR *(Psalms 90–106)*

PSALM 90

A prayer of Moses, the man of God.

¹Lord, through all the generations
>   you have been our home!
²Before the mountains were created,
>   before you made the earth and the world,
>   you are God, without beginning or end.

³You turn people back to dust, saying,
>   "Return to dust!"
⁴For you, a thousand years are as yesterday!
>   They are like a few hours!

[5]You sweep people away like dreams that disappear
    or like grass that springs up in the morning.
[6]In the morning it blooms and flourishes,
    but by evening it is dry and withered.
[7]We wither beneath your anger;
    we are overwhelmed by your fury.
[8]You spread out our sins before you—
    our secret sins—and you see them all.
[9]We live our lives beneath your wrath.
    We end our lives with a groan.

[10]Seventy years are given to us!
    Some may even reach eighty.
But even the best of these years are filled with pain and trouble;
    soon they disappear, and we are gone.
[11]Who can comprehend the power of your anger?
    Your wrath is as awesome as the fear you deserve.
[12]Teach us to make the most of our time,
    so that we may grow in wisdom.

[13]O LORD, come back to us!
    How long will you delay?
    Take pity on your servants!
[14]Satisfy us in the morning with your unfailing love,
    so we may sing for joy to the end of our lives.

¹⁵Give us gladness in proportion to our former misery!

    Replace the evil years with good.

¹⁶Let us see your miracles again;

    let our children see your glory at work.

¹⁷And may the Lord our God show us his approval

    and make our efforts successful.

    Yes, make our efforts successful!

PROVERBS 18

A recluse is self-indulgent, snarling at every sound principle of conduct.

²Fools have no interest in understanding; they only want to air their own opinions.

³When the wicked arrive, contempt, shame, and disgrace are sure to follow.

⁴A person's words can be life-giving water; words of true wisdom are as refreshing as a bubbling brook.

⁵It is wrong for a judge to favor the guilty or condemn the innocent.

⁶Fools get into constant quarrels; they are asking for a beating.

⁷The mouths of fools are their ruin; their lips get them into trouble.

⁸What dainty morsels rumors are—but they sink deep into one's heart.

⁹A lazy person is as bad as someone who destroys things.

¹⁰The name of the LORD is a strong fortress; the godly run to him and are safe.

¹¹The rich think of their wealth as an impregnable defense; they imagine it is a high wall of safety.

¹²Haughtiness goes before destruction; humility precedes honor.

¹³What a shame, what folly, to give advice before listening to the facts!

¹⁴The human spirit can endure a sick body, but who can bear it if the spirit is crushed?

¹⁵Intelligent people are always open to new ideas. In fact, they look for them.

¹⁶Giving a gift works wonders; it may bring you before important people!

¹⁷Any story sounds true until someone sets the record straight.

¹⁸Casting lots can end arguments and settle disputes between powerful opponents.

¹⁹It's harder to make amends with an offended friend

than to capture a fortified city. Arguments separate friends like a gate locked with iron bars.

²⁰Words satisfy the soul as food satisfies the stomach; the right words on a person's lips bring satisfaction.

²¹Those who love to talk will experience the consequences, for the tongue can kill or nourish life.

²²The man who finds a wife finds a treasure and receives favor from the LORD.

²³The poor plead for mercy; the rich answer with insults.

²⁴There are "friends" who destroy each other, but a real friend sticks closer than a brother.

DAY NINETEEN

PSALM 91

¹Those who live in the shelter of the Most High
    will find rest in the shadow of the Almighty.
²This I declare of the LORD:
    He alone is my refuge, my place of safety;
    he is my God, and I am trusting him.
³For he will rescue you from every trap
    and protect you from the fatal plague.
⁴He will shield you with his wings.
    He will shelter you with his feathers.
    His faithful promises are your armor and
        protection.
⁵Do not be afraid of the terrors of the night,
    nor fear the dangers of the day,
⁶nor dread the plague that stalks in darkness,
    nor the disaster that strikes at midday.
⁷Though a thousand fall at your side,
    though ten thousand are dying around you,
    these evils will not touch you.

⁸But you will see it with your eyes;
  you will see how the wicked are punished.

⁹If you make the LORD your refuge,
  if you make the Most High your shelter,
¹⁰no evil will conquer you;
  no plague will come near your dwelling.
¹¹For he orders his angels
  to protect you wherever you go.
¹²They will hold you with their hands
  to keep you from striking your foot on a stone.
¹³You will trample down lions and poisonous snakes;
  you will crush fierce lions and serpents under
    your feet!

¹⁴The LORD says, "I will rescue those who love me.
  I will protect those who trust in my name.
¹⁵When they call on me, I will answer;
  I will be with them in trouble.
  I will rescue them and honor them.
¹⁶I will satisfy them with a long life
  and give them my salvation."

A psalm to be sung on the LORD's Day. A song.

¹It is good to give thanks to the LORD,
   to sing praises to the Most High.
²It is good to proclaim your unfailing love in the morning,
   your faithfulness in the evening,
³accompanied by the harp and lute
   and the harmony of the lyre.
⁴You thrill me, LORD, with all you have done for me!
   I sing for joy because of what you have done.

⁵O LORD, what great miracles you do!
   And how deep are your thoughts.
⁶Only an ignorant person would not know this!
   Only a fool would not understand it.
⁷Although the wicked flourish like weeds,
   and evildoers blossom with success,
      there is only eternal destruction ahead of them.
⁸But you are exalted in the heavens.
   You, O LORD, continue forever.
⁹Your enemies, LORD, will surely perish;
   all evildoers will be scattered.

¹⁰But you have made me as strong as a wild bull.
   How refreshed I am by your power!

¹¹With my own eyes I have seen the downfall of my enemies;
    with my own ears I have heard the defeat of my
        wicked opponents.
¹²But the godly will flourish like palm trees
    and grow strong like the cedars of Lebanon.
¹³For they are transplanted into the LORD's own house.
    They flourish in the courts of our God.
¹⁴Even in old age they will still produce fruit;
    they will remain vital and green.
¹⁵They will declare, "The LORD is just!
    He is my rock!
    There is nothing but goodness in him!"

PSALM 93

¹The LORD is king! He is robed in majesty.
    Indeed, the LORD is robed in majesty and armed with
        strength.
The world is firmly established;
    it cannot be shaken.

²Your throne, O LORD, has been established from time
        immemorial.
    You yourself are from the everlasting past.

³The mighty oceans have roared, O LORD.

 The mighty oceans roar like thunder;

 the mighty oceans roar as they pound the shore.

⁴But mightier than the violent raging of the seas,

 mightier than the breakers on the shore—

 the LORD above is mightier than these!

⁵Your royal decrees cannot be changed.

 The nature of your reign, O LORD, is holiness forever.

PSALM 94

¹O LORD, the God to whom vengeance belongs,

 O God of vengeance, let your glorious justice be seen!

²Arise, O judge of the earth.

 Sentence the proud to the penalties they deserve.

³How long, O LORD?

 How long will the wicked be allowed to gloat?

⁴Hear their arrogance!

 How these evildoers boast!

⁵They oppress your people, LORD,

 hurting those you love.

⁶They kill widows and foreigners

 and murder orphans.

⁷"The LORD isn't looking," they say,

 "and besides, the God of Israel doesn't care."

⁸Think again, you fools!

When will you finally catch on?

⁹Is the one who made your ears deaf?

Is the one who formed your eyes blind?

¹⁰He punishes the nations—won't he also punish you?

He knows everything—doesn't he also know what

you are doing?

¹¹The LORD knows people's thoughts,

that they are worthless!

¹²Happy are those whom you discipline, LORD,

and those whom you teach from your law.

¹³You give them relief from troubled times

until a pit is dug for the wicked.

¹⁴The LORD will not reject his people;

he will not abandon his own special possession.

¹⁵Judgment will come again for the righteous,

and those who are upright will have a reward.

¹⁶Who will protect me from the wicked?

Who will stand up for me against evildoers?

¹⁷Unless the LORD had helped me,

I would soon have died.

¹⁸I cried out, "I'm slipping!"

and your unfailing love, O LORD, supported me.

¹⁹When doubts filled my mind,

    your comfort gave me renewed hope and cheer.

²⁰Can unjust leaders claim that God is on their side—

    leaders who permit injustice by their laws?

²¹They attack the righteous

    and condemn the innocent to death.

²²But the LORD is my fortress;

    my God is a mighty rock where I can hide.

²³God will make the sins of evil people fall back upon them.

    He will destroy them for their sins.

    The LORD our God will destroy them.

PSALM 95

¹Come, let us sing to the LORD!

    Let us give a joyous shout to the rock of our
        salvation!

²Let us come before him with thanksgiving.

    Let us sing him psalms of praise.

³For the LORD is a great God,

    the great King above all gods.

⁴He owns the depths of the earth,

    and even the mightiest mountains are his.

⁵The sea belongs to him, for he made it.

    His hands formed the dry land, too.

⁶Come, let us worship and bow down.

Let us kneel before the LORD our maker,

⁷   for he is our God.

We are the people he watches over,

the sheep under his care.

Oh, that you would listen to his voice today!

⁸The LORD says, "Don't harden your hearts as Israel did at Meribah,

as they did at Massah in the wilderness.

⁹For there your ancestors tried my patience;

they courted my wrath though they had seen my many miracles.

¹⁰For forty years I was angry with them, and I said,

'They are a people whose hearts turn away from me.

They refuse to do what I tell them.'

¹¹So in my anger I made a vow:

'They will never enter my place of rest.' "

PROVERBS 19

It is better to be poor and honest than to be a fool and dishonest.

²Zeal without knowledge is not good; a person who moves too quickly may go the wrong way.

³People ruin their lives by their own foolishness and then are angry at the LORD.

⁴Wealth makes many "friends"; poverty drives them away.

⁵A false witness will not go unpunished, nor will a liar escape.

⁶Many beg favors from a prince; everyone is the friend of a person who gives gifts!

⁷If the relatives of the poor despise them, how much more will their friends avoid them. The poor call after them, but they are gone.

⁸To acquire wisdom is to love oneself; people who cherish understanding will prosper.

⁹A false witness will not go unpunished, and a liar will be destroyed.

¹⁰It isn't right for a fool to live in luxury or for a slave to rule over princes!

¹¹People with good sense restrain their anger; they earn esteem by overlooking wrongs.

¹²The king's anger is like a lion's roar, but his favor is like dew on the grass.

¹³A foolish child is a calamity to a father; a nagging wife annoys like a constant dripping.

¹⁴Parents can provide their sons with an inheritance of

houses and wealth, but only the LORD can give an under-standing wife.

¹⁵A lazy person sleeps soundly—and goes hungry.

¹⁶Keep the commandments and keep your life; despising them leads to death.

¹⁷If you help the poor, you are lending to the LORD—and he will repay you!

¹⁸Discipline your children while there is hope. If you don't, you will ruin their lives.

¹⁹Short-tempered people must pay their own penalty. If you rescue them once, you will have to do it again.

²⁰Get all the advice and instruction you can, and be wise the rest of your life.

²¹You can make many plans, but the LORD's purpose will prevail.

²²Loyalty makes a person attractive. And it is better to be poor than dishonest.

²³Fear of the LORD gives life, security, and protection from harm.

²⁴Some people are so lazy that they won't even lift a finger to feed themselves.

²⁵If you punish a mocker, the simpleminded will learn a lesson; if you reprove the wise, they will be all the wiser.

²⁶Children who mistreat their father or chase away their mother are a public disgrace and an embarrassment.

²⁷If you stop listening to instruction, my child, you have turned your back on knowledge.

²⁸A corrupt witness makes a mockery of justice; the mouth of the wicked gulps down evil.

²⁹Mockers will be punished, and the backs of fools will be beaten.

DAY TWENTY

PSALM 96

¹Sing a new song to the LORD!
   Let the whole earth sing to the LORD!
²Sing to the LORD; bless his name.
   Each day proclaim the good news that he saves.
³Publish his glorious deeds among the nations.
   Tell everyone about the amazing things he does.
⁴Great is the LORD! He is most worthy of praise!
   He is to be revered above all the gods.
⁵The gods of other nations are merely idols,
   but the LORD made the heavens!
⁶Honor and majesty surround him;
   strength and beauty are in his sanctuary.

⁷O nations of the world, recognize the LORD;
   recognize that the LORD is glorious and strong.
⁸Give to the LORD the glory he deserves!
   Bring your offering and come to worship him.

⁹Worship the L<small>ORD</small> in all his holy splendor.

    Let all the earth tremble before him.

¹⁰Tell all the nations that the L<small>ORD</small> is king.

    The world is firmly established and cannot be
        shaken.

    He will judge all peoples fairly.

¹¹Let the heavens be glad, and let the earth rejoice!

    Let the sea and everything in it shout his praise!

12   Let the fields and their crops burst forth with joy!

    Let the trees of the forest rustle with praise

13   before the L<small>ORD</small>!

For the L<small>ORD</small> is coming!

    He is coming to judge the earth.

He will judge the world with righteousness

    and all the nations with his truth.

P<small>SALM</small> 97

¹The L<small>ORD</small> is king! Let the earth rejoice!

    Let the farthest islands be glad.

²Clouds and darkness surround him.

    Righteousness and justice are the foundation of his
        throne.

³Fire goes forth before him
    and burns up all his foes.
⁴His lightning flashes out across the world.
    The earth sees and trembles.
⁵The mountains melt like wax before the LORD,
    before the Lord of all the earth.
⁶The heavens declare his righteousness;
    every nation sees his glory.
⁷Those who worship idols are disgraced—
    all who brag about their worthless gods—
    for every god must bow to him.
⁸Jerusalem has heard and rejoiced,
    and all the cities of Judah are glad
    because of your justice, LORD!
⁹For you, O LORD, are most high over all the earth;
    you are exalted far above all gods.

¹⁰You who love the LORD, hate evil!
    He protects the lives of his godly people
    and rescues them from the power of the wicked.
¹¹Light shines on the godly,
    and joy on those who do right.
¹²May all who are godly be happy in the LORD
    and praise his holy name!

PSALM 98

A psalm.

¹Sing a new song to the LORD,
  for he has done wonderful deeds.
He has won a mighty victory
  by his power and holiness.
²The LORD has announced his victory
  and has revealed his righteousness to every nation!
³He has remembered his promise to love and be faithful to
      Israel.
  The whole earth has seen the salvation of our God.

⁴Shout to the LORD, all the earth;
  break out in praise and sing for joy!
⁵Sing your praise to the LORD with the harp,
  with the harp and melodious song,
⁶   with trumpets and the sound of the ram's horn.
Make a joyful symphony before the LORD, the King!

⁷Let the sea and everything in it shout his praise!
  Let the earth and all living things join in.
⁸   Let the rivers clap their hands in glee!
  Let the hills sing out their songs of joy
⁹   before the LORD.

For the LORD is coming to judge the earth.
    He will judge the world with justice,
    and the nations with fairness.

PSALM 99

¹The LORD is king!
    Let the nations tremble!
He sits on his throne between the cherubim.
    Let the whole earth quake!
²The LORD sits in majesty in Jerusalem,
    supreme above all the nations.
³Let them praise your great and awesome name.
    Your name is holy!
⁴Mighty king, lover of justice,
    you have established fairness.
You have acted with justice
    and righteousness throughout Israel.
⁵Exalt the LORD our God!
    Bow low before his feet, for he is holy!

⁶Moses and Aaron were among his priests;
    Samuel also called on his name.
They cried to the LORD for help,
    and he answered them.

⁷He spoke to them from the pillar of cloud,

and they followed the decrees and principles he gave
them.

⁸O LORD our God, you answered them.

You were a forgiving God,

but you punished them when they went wrong.

⁹Exalt the LORD our God

and worship at his holy mountain in Jerusalem,

for the LORD our God is holy!

PSALM 100

A psalm of thanksgiving.

¹Shout with joy to the LORD, O earth!

2   Worship the LORD with gladness.

Come before him, singing with joy.

³Acknowledge that the LORD is God!

He made us, and we are his.

We are his people, the sheep of his pasture.

⁴Enter his gates with thanksgiving;

go into his courts with praise.

Give thanks to him and bless his name.

⁵For the LORD is good.

His unfailing love continues forever,
and his faithfulness continues to each generation.

Wine produces mockers; liquor leads to brawls. Whoever is led astray by drink cannot be wise.

²The king's fury is like a lion's roar; to rouse his anger is to risk your life.

³Avoiding a fight is a mark of honor; only fools insist on quarreling.

⁴If you are too lazy to plow in the right season, you will have no food at the harvest.

⁵Though good advice lies deep within a person's heart, the wise will draw it out.

⁶Many will say they are loyal friends, but who can find one who is really faithful?

⁷The godly walk with integrity; blessed are their children after them.

⁸When a king judges, he carefully weighs all the evidence, distinguishing the bad from the good.

⁹Who can say, "I have cleansed my heart; I am pure and free from sin"?

¹⁰The LORD despises double standards of every kind.

¹¹Even children are known by the way they act, whether their conduct is pure and right.

¹²Ears to hear and eyes to see—both are gifts from the LORD.

¹³If you love sleep, you will end in poverty. Keep your eyes open, and there will be plenty to eat!

¹⁴The buyer haggles over the price, saying, "It's worthless," then brags about getting a bargain!

¹⁵Wise speech is rarer and more valuable than gold and rubies.

¹⁶Be sure to get collateral from anyone who guarantees the debt of a stranger. Get a deposit if someone guarantees the debt of a foreigner.

¹⁷Stolen bread tastes sweet, but it turns to gravel in the mouth.

¹⁸Plans succeed through good counsel; don't go to war without the advice of others.

¹⁹A gossip tells secrets, so don't hang around with someone who talks too much.

²⁰If you curse your father or mother, the lamp of your life will be snuffed out.

²¹An inheritance obtained early in life is not a blessing in the end.

²²Don't say, "I will get even for this wrong." Wait for the LORD to handle the matter.

²³The LORD despises double standards; he is not pleased by dishonest scales.

²⁴How can we understand the road we travel? It is the LORD who directs our steps.

²⁵It is dangerous to make a rash promise to God before counting the cost.

²⁶A wise king finds the wicked, lays them out like wheat, then runs the crushing wheel over them.

²⁷The LORD's searchlight penetrates the human spirit, exposing every hidden motive.

²⁸Unfailing love and faithfulness protect the king; his throne is made secure through love.

²⁹The glory of the young is their strength; the gray hair of experience is the splendor of the old.

³⁰Physical punishment cleanses away evil; such discipline purifies the heart.

DAY TWENTY-ONE

PSALM 101

A psalm of David.

¹I will sing of your love and justice.
  I will praise you, LORD, with songs.
²I will be careful to live a blameless life—
  when will you come to my aid?
I will lead a life of integrity
  in my own home.
³I will refuse to look at
  anything vile and vulgar.
I hate all crooked dealings;
  I will have nothing to do with them.
⁴I will reject perverse ideas
  and stay away from every evil.
⁵I will not tolerate people who slander their neighbors.
  I will not endure conceit and pride.

⁶I will keep a protective eye on the godly,
  so they may dwell with me in safety.

Only those who are above reproach
    will be allowed to serve me.
⁷I will not allow deceivers to serve me,
    and liars will not be allowed to enter my presence.
⁸My daily task will be to ferret out criminals
    and free the city of the LORD from their grip.

PSALM 102

*A prayer of one overwhelmed with trouble, pouring out problems before
the LORD.*

¹LORD, hear my prayer!
    Listen to my plea!
²Don't turn away from me
    in my time of distress.
Bend down your ear
    and answer me quickly when I call to you,
³   for my days disappear like smoke,
    and my bones burn like red-hot coals.
⁴My heart is sick, withered like grass,
    and I have lost my appetite.
⁵Because of my groaning,
    I am reduced to skin and bones.
⁶I am like an owl in the desert,
    like a lonely owl in a far-off wilderness.

⁷I lie awake,

  lonely as a solitary bird on the roof.
⁸My enemies taunt me day after day.

  They mock and curse me.
⁹I eat ashes instead of my food.

  My tears run down into my drink
¹⁰because of your anger and wrath.

  For you have picked me up and thrown me out.
¹¹My life passes as swiftly as the evening shadows.

  I am withering like grass.

¹²But you, O LORD, will rule forever.

  Your fame will endure to every generation.
¹³You will arise and have mercy on Jerusalem—

  and now is the time to pity her,

  now is the time you promised to help.
¹⁴For your people love every stone in her walls

  and show favor even to the dust in her streets.
¹⁵And the nations will tremble before the LORD.

  The kings of the earth will tremble before his glory.
¹⁶For the LORD will rebuild Jerusalem.

  He will appear in his glory.
¹⁷He will listen to the prayers of the destitute.

  He will not reject their pleas.

^{18}Let this be recorded for future generations,
>   so that a nation yet to be created will praise the
>   LORD.
^{19}Tell them the LORD looked down
>   from his heavenly sanctuary.
He looked to the earth from heaven
^{20} to hear the groans of the prisoners,
>   to release those condemned to die.
^{21}And so the LORD's fame will be celebrated in Zion,
>   his praises in Jerusalem,
^{22}when multitudes gather together
>   and kingdoms come to worship the LORD.

^{23}He has cut me down in midlife,
>   shortening my days.
^{24}But I cried to him, "My God, who lives forever,
>   don't take my life while I am still so young!
^{25}In ages past you laid the foundation of the earth,
>   and the heavens are the work of your hands.
^{26}Even they will perish, but you remain forever;
>   they will wear out like old clothing.
You will change them like a garment,
>   and they will fade away.
^{27}But you are always the same;
>   your years never end.

²⁸The children of your people
  will live in security.
Their children's children
  will thrive in your presence."

PSALM 103

A psalm of David.

¹Praise the LORD, I tell myself;
  with my whole heart, I will praise his holy name.
²Praise the LORD, I tell myself,
  and never forget the good things he does for me.
³He forgives all my sins
  and heals all my diseases.
⁴He ransoms me from death
  and surrounds me with love and tender mercies.
⁵He fills my life with good things.
  My youth is renewed like the eagle's!
⁶The LORD gives righteousness
  and justice to all who are treated unfairly.
⁷He revealed his character to Moses
  and his deeds to the people of Israel.
⁸The LORD is merciful and gracious;
  he is slow to get angry and full of unfailing love.

⁹He will not constantly accuse us,
nor remain angry forever.
¹⁰He has not punished us for all our sins,
nor does he deal with us as we deserve.
¹¹For his unfailing love toward those who fear him
is as great as the height of the heavens above the earth.
¹²He has removed our rebellious acts
as far away from us as the east is from the west.
¹³The LORD is like a father to his children,
tender and compassionate to those who fear him.
¹⁴For he understands how weak we are;
he knows we are only dust.
¹⁵Our days on earth are like grass;
like wildflowers, we bloom and die.
¹⁶The wind blows, and we are gone—
as though we had never been here.
¹⁷But the love of the LORD remains forever
with those who fear him.
His salvation extends to the children's children
18   of those who are faithful to his covenant,
of those who obey his commandments!

¹⁹The LORD has made the heavens his throne;
from there he rules over everything.
²⁰Praise the LORD, you angels of his,

you mighty creatures who carry out his plans,
listening for each of his commands.
²¹Yes, praise the LORD, you armies of angels
who serve him and do his will!
²²Praise the LORD, everything he has created,
everywhere in his kingdom.
As for me—I, too, will praise the LORD.

PROVERBS 21

The king's heart is like a stream of water directed by the LORD; he turns it wherever he pleases.

²People may think they are doing what is right, but the LORD examines the heart.

³The LORD is more pleased when we do what is just and right than when we give him sacrifices.

⁴Haughty eyes, a proud heart, and evil actions are all sin.

⁵Good planning and hard work lead to prosperity, but hasty shortcuts lead to poverty.

⁶Wealth created by lying is a vanishing mist and a deadly trap.

⁷Because the wicked refuse to do what is just, their violence boomerangs and destroys them.

⁸The guilty walk a crooked path; the innocent travel a straight road.

⁹It is better to live alone in the corner of an attic than with a contentious wife in a lovely home.

¹⁰Evil people love to harm others; their neighbors get no mercy from them.

¹¹A simpleton can learn only by seeing mockers punished; a wise person learns from instruction.

¹²The Righteous One knows what is going on in the homes of the wicked; he will bring the wicked to disaster.

¹³Those who shut their ears to the cries of the poor will be ignored in their own time of need.

¹⁴A secret gift calms anger; a secret bribe pacifies fury.

¹⁵Justice is a joy to the godly, but it causes dismay among evildoers.

¹⁶The person who strays from common sense will end up in the company of the dead.

¹⁷Those who love pleasure become poor; wine and luxury are not the way to riches.

¹⁸Sometimes the wicked are punished to save the godly, and the treacherous for the upright.

¹⁹It is better to live alone in the desert than with a crabby, complaining wife.

^{20}The wise have wealth and luxury, but fools spend whatever they get.

^{21}Whoever pursues godliness and unfailing love will find life, godliness, and honor.

^{22}The wise conquer the city of the strong and level the fortress in which they trust.

^{23}If you keep your mouth shut, you will stay out of trouble.

^{24}Mockers are proud and haughty; they act with boundless arrogance.

^{25}The desires of lazy people will be their ruin, for their hands refuse to work. ^{26}They are always greedy for more, while the godly love to give!

^{27}God loathes the sacrifice of an evil person, especially when it is brought with ulterior motives.

^{28}A false witness will be cut off, but an attentive witness will be allowed to speak.

^{29}The wicked put up a bold front, but the upright proceed with care.

^{30}Human plans, no matter how wise or well advised, cannot stand against the LORD.

^{31}The horses are prepared for battle, but the victory belongs to the LORD.

DAY TWENTY-TWO

PSALM 104

¹Praise the LORD, I tell myself;
O LORD my God, how great you are!
You are robed with honor and with majesty;
  ² you are dressed in a robe of light.
You stretch out the starry curtain of the heavens;
  ³ you lay out the rafters of your home in the rain
      clouds.
You make the clouds your chariots;
  you ride upon the wings of the wind.
⁴The winds are your messengers;
  flames of fire are your servants.

⁵You placed the world on its foundation
  so it would never be moved.
⁶You clothed the earth with floods of water,
  water that covered even the mountains.
⁷At the sound of your rebuke, the water fled;
  at the sound of your thunder, it fled away.

⁸Mountains rose and valleys sank
    to the levels you decreed.
⁹Then you set a firm boundary for the seas,
    so they would never again cover the earth.

¹⁰You make the springs pour water into ravines,
    so streams gush down from the mountains.
¹¹They provide water for all the animals,
    and the wild donkeys quench their thirst.
¹²The birds nest beside the streams
    and sing among the branches of the trees.
¹³You send rain on the mountains from your heavenly home,
    and you fill the earth with the fruit of your labor.
¹⁴You cause grass to grow for the cattle.
    You cause plants to grow for people to use.
You allow them to produce food from the earth—
¹⁵   wine to make them glad,
    olive oil as lotion for their skin,
    and bread to give them strength.
¹⁶The trees of the LORD are well cared for—
    the cedars of Lebanon that he planted.
¹⁷There the birds make their nests,
    and the storks make their homes in the firs.
¹⁸High in the mountains are pastures for the wild goats,
    and the rocks form a refuge for rock badgers.

[19]You made the moon to mark the seasons
 and the sun that knows when to set.
[20]You send the darkness, and it becomes night,
 when all the forest animals prowl about.
[21]Then the young lions roar for their food,
 but they are dependent on God.
[22]At dawn they slink back
 into their dens to rest.
[23]Then people go off to their work;
 they labor until the evening shadows fall again.

[24]O LORD, what a variety of things you have made!
 In wisdom you have made them all.
 The earth is full of your creatures.
[25]Here is the ocean, vast and wide,
 teeming with life of every kind,
 both great and small.
[26]See the ships sailing along,
 and Leviathan, which you made to play in the sea.
[27]Every one of these depends on you
 to give them their food as they need it.
[28]When you supply it, they gather it.
 You open your hand to feed them, and they are
  satisfied.
[29]But if you turn away from them, they panic.

When you take away their breath, they die
   and turn again to dust.
³⁰When you send your Spirit, new life is born
   to replenish all the living of the earth.

³¹May the glory of the LORD last forever!
   The LORD rejoices in all he has made!
³²The earth trembles at his glance;
   the mountains burst into flame at his touch.
³³I will sing to the LORD as long as I live.
   I will praise my God to my last breath!
³⁴May he be pleased by all these thoughts about him,
   for I rejoice in the LORD.
³⁵Let all sinners vanish from the face of the earth;
   let the wicked disappear forever.
As for me—I will praise the LORD!

Praise the LORD!

PSALM 105

¹Give thanks to the LORD and proclaim his greatness.
   Let the whole world know what he has done.
²Sing to him; yes, sing his praises.
   Tell everyone about his miracles.

³Exult in his holy name;

O worshipers of the LORD, rejoice!

⁴Search for the LORD and for his strength,

and keep on searching.

⁵Think of the wonderful works he has done,

the miracles and the judgments he handed down,

⁶O children of Abraham, God's servant,

O descendants of Jacob, God's chosen one.

⁷He is the LORD our God.

His rule is seen throughout the land.

⁸He always stands by his covenant—

the commitment he made to a thousand generations.

⁹This is the covenant he made with Abraham

and the oath he swore to Isaac.

¹⁰He confirmed it to Jacob as a decree,

to the people of Israel as a never-ending treaty:

¹¹"I will give you the land of Canaan

as your special possession."

¹²He said this when they were few in number,

a tiny group of strangers in Canaan.

¹³They wandered back and forth between nations,

from one kingdom to another.

¹⁴Yet he did not let anyone oppress them.

He warned kings on their behalf:

¹⁵"Do not touch these people I have chosen,
  and do not hurt my prophets."
¹⁶He called for a famine on the land of Canaan,
  cutting off its food supply.
¹⁷Then he sent someone to Egypt ahead of them—
  Joseph, who was sold as a slave.
¹⁸There in prison, they bruised his feet with fetters
  and placed his neck in an iron collar.
¹⁹Until the time came to fulfill his word,
  the LORD tested Joseph's character.
²⁰Then Pharaoh sent for him and set him free;
  the ruler of the nation opened his prison door.
²¹Joseph was put in charge of all the king's household;
  he became ruler over all the king's possessions.
²²He could instruct the king's aides as he pleased
  and teach the king's advisers.

²³Then Israel arrived in Egypt;
  Jacob lived as a foreigner in the land of Ham.
²⁴And the LORD multiplied the people of Israel
  until they became too mighty for their enemies.
²⁵Then he turned the Egyptians against the Israelites,
  and they plotted against the LORD's servants.

²⁶But the LORD sent Moses his servant,
  along with Aaron, whom he had chosen.

²⁷They performed miraculous signs among the Egyptians,
　　and miracles in the land of Ham.
²⁸The LORD blanketed Egypt in darkness,
　　for they had defied his commands to let his people go.
²⁹He turned the nation's water into blood,
　　poisoning all the fish.
³⁰Then frogs overran the land;
　　they were found even in the king's private rooms.
³¹When he spoke, flies descended on the Egyptians,
　　and gnats swarmed across Egypt.
³²Instead of rain, he sent murderous hail,
　　and flashes of lightning overwhelmed the land.
³³He ruined their grapevines and fig trees
　　and shattered all the trees.
³⁴He spoke, and hordes of locusts came—
　　locusts beyond number.
³⁵They ate up everything green in the land,
　　destroying all the crops.
³⁶Then he killed the oldest child in each Egyptian home,
　　the pride and joy of each family.

³⁷But he brought his people safely out of Egypt, loaded
　　with silver and gold;
　　there were no sick or feeble people among them.

³⁸Egypt was glad when they were gone,
  for the dread of them was great.
³⁹The LORD spread out a cloud above them as a covering
  and gave them a great fire to light the darkness.
⁴⁰They asked for meat, and he sent them quail;
  he gave them manna—bread from heaven.
⁴¹He opened up a rock, and water gushed out
  to form a river through the dry and barren land.
⁴²For he remembered his sacred promise
  to Abraham his servant.
⁴³So he brought his people out of Egypt with joy,
  his chosen ones with rejoicing.
⁴⁴He gave his people the lands of pagan nations,
  and they harvested crops that others had planted.
⁴⁵All this happened so they would follow his principles
  and obey his laws.

Praise the LORD!

PROVERBS 22

Choose a good reputation over great riches, for being held in high esteem is better than having silver or gold.

²The rich and the poor have this in common: The LORD made them both.

³A prudent person foresees the danger ahead and takes

precautions; the simpleton goes blindly on and suffers the consequences.

⁴True humility and fear of the LORD lead to riches, honor, and long life.

⁵The deceitful walk a thorny, treacherous road; whoever values life will stay away.

⁶Teach your children to choose the right path, and when they are older, they will remain upon it.

⁷Just as the rich rule the poor, so the borrower is servant to the lender.

⁸Those who plant seeds of injustice will harvest disaster, and their reign of terror will end.

⁹Blessed are those who are generous, because they feed the poor.

¹⁰Throw out the mocker, and fighting, quarrels, and insults will disappear.

¹¹Anyone who loves a pure heart and gracious speech is the king's friend.

¹²The LORD preserves knowledge, but he ruins the plans of the deceitful.

¹³The lazy person is full of excuses, saying, "If I go outside, I might meet a lion in the street and be killed!"

¹⁴The mouth of an immoral woman is a deep pit; those living under the LORD's displeasure will fall into it.

¹⁵A youngster's heart is filled with foolishness, but discipline will drive it away.

¹⁶A person who gets ahead by oppressing the poor or by showering gifts on the rich will end in poverty.

¹⁷Listen to the words of the wise; apply your heart to my instruction. ¹⁸For it is good to keep these sayings deep within yourself, always ready on your lips. ¹⁹I am teaching you today—yes, you—so you will trust in the Lord. ²⁰I have written thirty sayings for you, filled with advice and knowledge. ²¹In this way, you may know the truth and bring an accurate report to those who sent you.

²²Do not rob the poor because they are poor or exploit the needy in court. ²³For the Lord is their defender. He will injure anyone who injures them.

²⁴Keep away from angry, short-tempered people, ²⁵or you will learn to be like them and endanger your soul.

²⁶Do not co-sign another person's note or put up a guarantee for someone else's loan. ²⁷If you can't pay it, even your bed will be snatched from under you.

²⁸Do not steal your neighbor's property by moving the ancient boundary markers set up by your ancestors.

²⁹Do you see any truly competent workers? They will serve kings rather than ordinary people.

DAY TWENTY-THREE

PSALM 106

¹Praise the LORD!

Give thanks to the LORD, for he is good!
　　His faithful love endures forever.
²Who can list the glorious miracles of the LORD?
　　Who can ever praise him half enough?
³Happy are those who deal justly with others
　　and always do what is right.

⁴Remember me, too, LORD, when you show favor to your
　　　　people;
　　come to me with your salvation.
⁵Let me share in the prosperity of your chosen ones.
　　Let me rejoice in the joy of your people;
　　let me praise you with those who are your heritage.

⁶Both we and our ancestors have sinned.
　　We have done wrong! We have acted wickedly!

⁷Our ancestors in Egypt
    were not impressed by the LORD's miracles.
They soon forgot his many acts of kindness to them.
    Instead, they rebelled against him at the Red Sea.
⁸Even so, he saved them—
    to defend the honor of his name
    and to demonstrate his mighty power.
⁹He commanded the Red Sea to divide, and a dry path
        appeared.
    He led Israel across the sea bottom that was as dry
        as a desert.
¹⁰So he rescued them from their enemies
    and redeemed them from their foes.
¹¹Then the water returned and covered their enemies;
    not one of them survived.
¹²Then at last his people believed his promises.
    Then they finally sang his praise.

¹³Yet how quickly they forgot what he had done!
    They wouldn't wait for his counsel!
¹⁴In the wilderness, their desires ran wild,
    testing God's patience in that dry land.
¹⁵So he gave them what they asked for,
    but he sent a plague along with it.

¹⁶The people in the camp were jealous of Moses
    and envious of Aaron, the LORD's holy priest.
¹⁷Because of this, the earth opened up;
    it swallowed Dathan
    and buried Abiram and the other rebels.
¹⁸Fire fell upon their followers;
    a flame consumed the wicked.

¹⁹The people made a calf at Mount Sinai;
    they bowed before an image made of gold.
²⁰They traded their glorious God
    for a statue of a grass-eating ox!
²¹They forgot God, their savior,
    who had done such great things in Egypt—
²²such wonderful things in that land,
    such awesome deeds at the Red Sea.
²³So he declared he would destroy them.
    But Moses, his chosen one, stepped between the LORD
        and the people.
    He begged him to turn from his anger and not destroy
        them.

²⁴The people refused to enter the pleasant land,
    for they wouldn't believe his promise to care for
        them.

²⁵Instead, they grumbled in their tents
  and refused to obey the LORD.
²⁶Therefore, he swore
  that he would kill them in the wilderness,
²⁷that he would scatter their descendants among the
    nations,
  exiling them to distant lands.

²⁸Then our ancestors joined in the worship of Baal at Peor;
  they even ate sacrifices offered to the dead!
²⁹They angered the LORD with all these things,
  so a plague broke out among them.
³⁰But Phinehas had the courage to step in,
  and the plague was stopped.
³¹So he has been regarded as a righteous man
  ever since that time.

³²At Meribah, too, they angered the LORD,
  causing Moses serious trouble.
³³They made Moses angry,
  and he spoke foolishly.

³⁴Israel failed to destroy the nations in the land,
  as the LORD had told them to.
³⁵Instead, they mingled among the pagans
  and adopted their evil customs.

³⁶They worshiped their idols,
  and this led to their downfall.
³⁷They even sacrificed their sons
  and their daughters to the demons.
³⁸They shed innocent blood,
  the blood of their sons and daughters.
By sacrificing them to the idols of Canaan,
  they polluted the land with murder.
³⁹They defiled themselves by their evil deeds,
  and their love of idols was adultery in the LORD's
    sight.

⁴⁰That is why the LORD's anger burned against his people,
  and he abhorred his own special possession.
⁴¹He handed them over to pagan nations,
  and those who hated them ruled over them.
⁴²Their enemies crushed them
  and brought them under their cruel power.
⁴³Again and again he delivered them,
  but they continued to rebel against him,
  and they were finally destroyed by their sin.
⁴⁴Even so, he pitied them in their distress
  and listened to their cries.
⁴⁵He remembered his covenant with them
  and relented because of his unfailing love.

⁴⁶He even caused their captors
   to treat them with kindness.

⁴⁷O Lord our God, save us!
   Gather us back from among the nations,
so we can thank your holy name
   and rejoice and praise you.

⁴⁸Blessed be the Lord, the God of Israel,
   from everlasting to everlasting!
Let all the people say, "Amen!"

Praise the Lord!

Book Five (Psalms 107–150)

PSALM 107

¹Give thanks to the Lord, for he is good!
   His faithful love endures forever.
²Has the Lord redeemed you? Then speak out!
   Tell others he has saved you from your enemies.
³For he has gathered the exiles from many lands,
   from east and west, from north and south.

⁴Some wandered in the desert,
   lost and homeless.

⁵Hungry and thirsty,
　　they nearly died.
⁶"LORD, help!" they cried in their trouble,
　　and he rescued them from their distress.
⁷He led them straight to safety,
　　to a city where they could live.
⁸Let them praise the LORD for his great love
　　and for all his wonderful deeds to them.
⁹For he satisfies the thirsty
　　and fills the hungry with good things.

¹⁰Some sat in darkness and deepest gloom,
　　miserable prisoners in chains.
¹¹They rebelled against the words of God,
　　scorning the counsel of the Most High.
¹²That is why he broke them with hard labor;
　　they fell, and no one helped them rise again.
¹³"LORD, help!" they cried in their trouble,
　　and he saved them from their distress.
¹⁴He led them from the darkness and deepest gloom;
　　he snapped their chains.
¹⁵Let them praise the LORD for his great love
　　and for all his wonderful deeds to them.
¹⁶For he broke down their prison gates of bronze;
　　he cut apart their bars of iron.

¹⁷Some were fools in their rebellion;
     they suffered for their sins.
¹⁸Their appetites were gone,
     and death was near.
¹⁹"LORD, help!" they cried in their trouble,
     and he saved them from their distress.
²⁰He spoke, and they were healed—
     snatched from the door of death.
²¹Let them praise the LORD for his great love
     and for all his wonderful deeds to them.
²²Let them offer sacrifices of thanksgiving
     and sing joyfully about his glorious acts.

²³Some went off in ships,
     plying the trade routes of the world.
²⁴They, too, observed the LORD's power in action,
     his impressive works on the deepest seas.
²⁵He spoke, and the winds rose,
     stirring up the waves.
²⁶Their ships were tossed to the heavens
     and sank again to the depths;
     the sailors cringed in terror.
²⁷They reeled and staggered like drunkards
     and were at their wits' end.

²⁸"LORD, help!" they cried in their trouble,
      and he saved them from their distress.
²⁹He calmed the storm to a whisper
      and stilled the waves.
³⁰What a blessing was that stillness
      as he brought them safely into harbor!
³¹Let them praise the LORD for his great love
      and for all his wonderful deeds to them.
³²Let them exalt him publicly before the congregation
      and before the leaders of the nation.

³³He changes rivers into deserts,
      and springs of water into dry land.
³⁴He turns the fruitful land into salty wastelands,
      because of the wickedness of those who live there.
³⁵But he also turns deserts into pools of water,
      the dry land into flowing springs.
³⁶He brings the hungry to settle there
      and build their cities.
³⁷They sow their fields, plant their vineyards,
      and harvest their bumper crops.
³⁸How he blesses them!
      They raise large families there,
      and their herds of cattle increase.

³⁹When they decrease in number and become
　　　impoverished
　　through oppression, trouble, and sorrow,
⁴⁰the LORD pours contempt on their princes,
　　causing them to wander in trackless wastelands.
⁴¹But he rescues the poor from their distress
　　and increases their families like vast flocks of sheep.
⁴²The godly will see these things and be glad,
　　while the wicked are stricken silent.
⁴³Those who are wise will take all this to heart;
　　they will see in our history the faithful love of the
　　　LORD.

PROVERBS 23

When dining with a ruler, pay attention to what is put
before you. ²If you are a big eater, put a knife to your
throat, ³and don't desire all the delicacies—deception may
be involved.

⁴Don't weary yourself trying to get rich. Why waste
your time? ⁵For riches can disappear as though they had the
wings of a bird!

⁶Don't eat with people who are stingy; don't desire
their delicacies. ⁷"Eat and drink," they say, but they don't
mean it. They are always thinking about how much it

costs. ⁸You will vomit up the delicious food they serve, and you will have to take back your words of appreciation for their "kindness."

⁹Don't waste your breath on fools, for they will despise the wisest advice.

¹⁰Don't steal the land of defenseless orphans by moving the ancient boundary markers, ¹¹for their Redeemer is strong. He himself will bring their charges against you.

¹²Commit yourself to instruction; attune your ears to hear words of knowledge.

¹³Don't fail to correct your children. They won't die if you spank them. ¹⁴Physical discipline may well save them from death.

¹⁵My child, how I will rejoice if you become wise. ¹⁶Yes, my heart will thrill when you speak what is right and just.

¹⁷Don't envy sinners, but always continue to fear the LORD. ¹⁸For surely you have a future ahead of you; your hope will not be disappointed.

¹⁹My child, listen and be wise. Keep your heart on the right course. ²⁰Do not carouse with drunkards and gluttons, ²¹for they are on their way to poverty. Too much sleep clothes a person with rags.

²²Listen to your father, who gave you life, and don't despise your mother's experience when she is old. ²³Get the truth and don't ever sell it; also get wisdom, discipline, and discernment. ²⁴The father of godly children has cause for joy. What a pleasure it is to have wise children. ²⁵So give your parents joy! May she who gave you birth be happy.

²⁶O my son, give me your heart. May your eyes delight in my ways of wisdom. ²⁷A prostitute is a deep pit; an adulterous woman is treacherous. ²⁸She hides and waits like a robber, looking for another victim who will be unfaithful to his wife.

²⁹Who has anguish? Who has sorrow? Who is always fighting? Who is always complaining? Who has unnecessary bruises? Who has bloodshot eyes? ³⁰It is the one who spends long hours in the taverns, trying out new drinks. ³¹Don't let the sparkle and smooth taste of wine deceive you. ³²For in the end it bites like a poisonous serpent; it stings like a viper. ³³You will see hallucinations, and you will say crazy things. ³⁴You will stagger like a sailor tossed at sea, clinging to a swaying mast. ³⁵And you will say, "They hit me, but I didn't feel it. I didn't even know it when they beat me up. When will I wake up so I can have another drink?"

DAY TWENTY-FOUR

PSALM 108

A psalm of David. A song.

¹My heart is confident in you, O God;
    no wonder I can sing your praises!
Wake up, my soul!
²   Wake up, O harp and lyre!
    I will waken the dawn with my song.
³I will thank you, LORD, in front of all the people.
    I will sing your praises among the nations.
⁴For your unfailing love is higher than the heavens.
    Your faithfulness reaches to the clouds.
⁵Be exalted, O God, above the highest heavens.
    May your glory shine over all the earth.

⁶Use your strong right arm to save me,
    and rescue your beloved people.
⁷God has promised this by his holiness:
    "I will divide up Shechem with joy.
    I will measure out the valley of Succoth.

⁸Gilead is mine,
>   and Manasseh is mine.
Ephraim will produce my warriors,
>   and Judah will produce my kings.
⁹Moab will become my lowly servant,
>   and Edom will be my slave.
>   I will shout in triumph over the Philistines."

¹⁰But who will bring me into the fortified city?
>   Who will bring me victory over Edom?
¹¹Have you rejected us, O God?
>   Will you no longer march with our armies?
¹²Oh, please help us against our enemies,
>   for all human help is useless.
¹³With God's help we will do mighty things,
>   for he will trample down our foes.

PSALM 109

For the choir director: A psalm of David.

¹O God, whom I praise,
>   don't stand silent and aloof
²while the wicked slander me
>   and tell lies about me.

³They are all around me with their hateful words,
  and they fight against me for no reason.
⁴I love them, but they try to destroy me—
  even as I am praying for them!
⁵They return evil for good,
  and hatred for my love.

⁶Arrange for an evil person to turn on him.
  Send an accuser to bring him to trial.
⁷When his case is called for judgment,
  let him be pronounced guilty.
  Count his prayers as sins.
⁸Let his years be few;
  let his position be given to someone else.
⁹May his children become fatherless,
  and may his wife become a widow.
¹⁰May his children wander as beggars;
  may they be evicted from their ruined homes.
¹¹May creditors seize his entire estate,
  and strangers take all he has earned.
¹²Let no one be kind to him;
  let no one pity his fatherless children.
¹³May all his offspring die.
  May his family name be blotted out in a single
    generation.

¹⁴May the LORD never forget the sins of his ancestors;
    may his mother's sins never be erased from the
        record.
¹⁵May these sins always remain before the LORD,
    but may his name be cut off from human memory.
¹⁶For he refused all kindness to others;
    he persecuted the poor and needy,
    and he hounded the brokenhearted to death.
¹⁷He loved to curse others;
    now you curse him.
He never blessed others;
    now don't you bless him.
¹⁸Cursing is as much a part of him as his clothing,
    or as the water he drinks,
    or the rich food he eats.
¹⁹Now may his curses return and cling to him like
        clothing;
    may they be tied around him like a belt.

²⁰May those curses become the LORD's punishment for my
        accusers
    who are plotting against my life.
²¹But deal well with me, O Sovereign LORD,
    for the sake of your own reputation!
Rescue me because you are so faithful and good.

²² For I am poor and needy,
   and my heart is full of pain.
²³I am fading like a shadow at dusk;
   I am falling like a grasshopper that is brushed aside.
²⁴My knees are weak from fasting,
   and I am skin and bones.
²⁵I am an object of mockery to people everywhere;
   when they see me, they shake their heads.

²⁶Help me, O LORD my God!
   Save me because of your unfailing love.
²⁷Let them see that this is your doing,
   that you yourself have done it, LORD.
²⁸Then let them curse me if they like,
   but you will bless me!
When they attack me, they will be disgraced!
   But I, your servant, will go right on rejoicing!
²⁹Make their humiliation obvious to all;
   clothe my accusers with disgrace.
³⁰But I will give repeated thanks to the LORD,
   praising him to everyone.
³¹For he stands beside the needy,
   ready to save them from those who condemn
      them.

A psalm of David.

¹The LORD said to my Lord,
  "Sit in honor at my right hand
until I humble your enemies,
  making them a footstool under your feet."

²The LORD will extend your powerful dominion from
    Jerusalem;
  you will rule over your enemies.
³In that day of battle,
  your people will serve you willingly.
Arrayed in holy garments,
  your vigor will be renewed each day like the morning
    dew.
⁴The LORD has taken an oath and will not break his vow:
  "You are a priest forever in the line of Melchizedek."
⁵The Lord stands at your right hand to protect you.
  He will strike down many kings in the day of his
    anger.
⁶He will punish the nations
  and fill them with their dead;
he will shatter heads
  over the whole earth.

⁷But he himself will be refreshed from brooks along the
way.

He will be victorious.

PSALM 111

¹Praise the LORD!

I will thank the LORD with all my heart
as I meet with his godly people.
²How amazing are the deeds of the LORD!
All who delight in him should ponder them.
³Everything he does reveals his glory and majesty.
His righteousness never fails.
⁴Who can forget the wonders he performs?
How gracious and merciful is our LORD!
⁵He gives food to those who trust him;
he always remembers his covenant.
⁶He has shown his great power to his people
by giving them the lands of other nations.
⁷All he does is just and good,
and all his commandments are trustworthy.
⁸They are forever true,
to be obeyed faithfully and with integrity.
⁹He has paid a full ransom for his people.

He has guaranteed his covenant with them forever.

What a holy, awe-inspiring name he has!

¹⁰Reverence for the LORD is the foundation of true
    wisdom.

The rewards of wisdom come to all who obey him.

Praise his name forever!

Don't envy evil people; don't desire their company. ²For
they spend their days plotting violence, and their words
are always stirring up trouble.

³A house is built by wisdom and becomes strong
through good sense. ⁴Through knowledge its rooms are
filled with all sorts of precious riches and valuables.

⁵A wise man is mightier than a strong man, and a man
of knowledge is more powerful than a strong man. ⁶So
don't go to war without wise guidance; victory depends
on having many counselors.

⁷Wisdom is too much for a fool. When the leaders
gather, the fool has nothing to say.

⁸A person who plans evil will get a reputation as a
troublemaker. ⁹The schemes of a fool are sinful; everyone
despises a mocker.

¹⁰If you fail under pressure, your strength is not very great.

¹¹Rescue those who are unjustly sentenced to death; don't stand back and let them die. ¹²Don't try to avoid responsibility by saying you didn't know about it. For God knows all hearts, and he sees you. He keeps watch over your soul, and he knows you knew! And he will judge all people according to what they have done.

¹³My child, eat honey, for it is good, and the honeycomb is sweet to the taste. ¹⁴In the same way, wisdom is sweet to your soul. If you find it, you will have a bright future, and your hopes will not be cut short.

¹⁵Do not lie in wait like an outlaw at the home of the godly. And don't raid the house where the godly live. ¹⁶They may trip seven times, but each time they will rise again. But one calamity is enough to lay the wicked low.

¹⁷Do not rejoice when your enemies fall into trouble. Don't be happy when they stumble. ¹⁸For the Lord will be displeased with you and will turn his anger away from them.

¹⁹Do not fret because of evildoers; don't envy the wicked. ²⁰For the evil have no future; their light will be snuffed out.

²¹My child, fear the Lord and the king, and don't

associate with rebels. ²²For you will go down with them to sudden disaster. Who knows where the punishment from the LORD and the king will end?

²³Here are some further sayings of the wise:

It is wrong to show favoritism when passing judgment. ²⁴A judge who says to the wicked, "You are innocent," will be cursed by many people and denounced by the nations. ²⁵But blessings are showered on those who convict the guilty.

²⁶It is an honor to receive an honest reply.

²⁷Develop your business first before building your house.

²⁸Do not testify spitefully against innocent neighbors; don't lie about them. ²⁹And don't say, "Now I can pay them back for all their meanness to me! I'll get even!"

³⁰I walked by the field of a lazy person, the vineyard of one lacking sense. ³¹I saw that it was overgrown with thorns. It was covered with weeds, and its walls were broken down. ³²Then, as I looked and thought about it, I learned this lesson: ³³A little extra sleep, a little more slumber, a little folding of the hands to rest—³⁴and poverty will pounce on you like a bandit; scarcity will attack you like an armed robber.

PSALM 112

¹Praise the LORD!

Happy are those who fear the LORD.
>   Yes, happy are those who delight in doing what he
>   commands.
²Their children will be successful everywhere;
>   an entire generation of godly people will be blessed.
³They themselves will be wealthy,
>   and their good deeds will never be forgotten.
⁴When darkness overtakes the godly, light will come
>   bursting in.
>   They are generous, compassionate, and righteous.
⁵All goes well for those who are generous,
>   who lend freely and conduct their business fairly.
⁶Such people will not be overcome by evil circumstances.
>   Those who are righteous will be long remembered.
⁷They do not fear bad news;
>   they confidently trust the LORD to care for them.

⁸They are confident and fearless
and can face their foes triumphantly.
⁹They give generously to those in need.
Their good deeds will never be forgotten.
They will have influence and honor.
¹⁰The wicked will be infuriated when they see this.
They will grind their teeth in anger;
they will slink away, their hopes thwarted.

PSALM 113

¹Praise the LORD!

Yes, give praise, O servants of the LORD.
Praise the name of the LORD!
²Blessed be the name of the LORD
forever and ever.
³Everywhere—from east to west—
praise the name of the LORD.
⁴For the LORD is high above the nations;
his glory is far greater than the heavens.

⁵Who can be compared with the LORD our God,
who is enthroned on high?
⁶Far below him are the heavens and the earth.
He stoops to look,

7and he lifts the poor from the dirt
　　and the needy from the garbage dump.
8He sets them among princes,
　　even the princes of his own people!
9He gives the barren woman a home,
　　so that she becomes a happy mother.

Praise the LORD!

PSALM 114

1When the Israelites escaped from Egypt—
　　when the family of Jacob left that foreign land—
2the land of Judah became God's sanctuary,
　　and Israel became his kingdom.

3The Red Sea saw them coming and hurried out of their
　　　way!
　　The water of the Jordan River turned away.
4The mountains skipped like rams,
　　the little hills like lambs!
5What's wrong, Red Sea, that made you hurry out of
　　　their way?
　　What happened, Jordan River, that you turned away?
6Why, mountains, did you skip like rams?
　　Why, little hills, like lambs?

⁷Tremble, O earth, at the presence of the Lord,
    at the presence of the God of Israel.
⁸He turned the rock into pools of water;
    yes, springs of water came from solid rock.

PSALM 115

¹Not to us, O LORD, but to you goes all the glory
    for your unfailing love and faithfulness.
²Why let the nations say,
    "Where is their God?"
³For our God is in the heavens,
    and he does as he wishes.
⁴Their idols are merely things of silver and gold,
    shaped by human hands.
⁵They cannot talk, though they have mouths,
    or see, though they have eyes!
⁶They cannot hear with their ears,
    or smell with their noses,
⁷   or feel with their hands,
    or walk with their feet,
    or utter sounds with their throats!
⁸And those who make them are just like them,
    as are all who trust in them.

⁹O Israel, trust the LORD!
　　He is your helper; he is your shield.
¹⁰O priests of Aaron, trust the LORD!
　　He is your helper; he is your shield.
¹¹All you who fear the LORD, trust the LORD!
　　He is your helper; he is your shield.

¹²The LORD remembers us,
　　and he will surely bless us.
He will bless the people of Israel
　　and the family of Aaron, the priests.
¹³He will bless those who fear the LORD,
　　both great and small.

¹⁴May the LORD richly bless
　　both you and your children.
¹⁵May you be blessed by the LORD,
　　who made heaven and earth.
¹⁶The heavens belong to the LORD,
　　but he has given the earth to all humanity.

¹⁷The dead cannot sing praises to the LORD,
　　for they have gone into the silence of the grave.
¹⁸But we can praise the LORD
　　both now and forever!

Praise the LORD!

¹I love the LORD because he hears
    and answers my prayers.
²Because he bends down and listens,
    I will pray as long as I have breath!
³Death had its hands around my throat;
    the terrors of the grave overtook me.
    I saw only trouble and sorrow.
⁴Then I called on the name of the LORD:
    "Please, LORD, save me!"
⁵How kind the LORD is! How good he is!
    So merciful, this God of ours!
⁶The LORD protects those of childlike faith;
    I was facing death, and then he saved me.
⁷Now I can rest again,
    for the LORD has been so good to me.
⁸He has saved me from death,
    my eyes from tears,
    my feet from stumbling.
⁹And so I walk in the LORD's presence
    as I live here on earth!
¹⁰I believed in you, so I prayed,
    "I am deeply troubled, LORD."
¹¹In my anxiety I cried out to you,

"These people are all liars!"
¹²What can I offer the LORD
	for all he has done for me?
¹³I will lift up a cup symbolizing his salvation;
	I will praise the LORD's name for saving me.
¹⁴I will keep my promises to the LORD
	in the presence of all his people.

¹⁵The LORD's loved ones are precious to him;
	it grieves him when they die.
¹⁶O LORD, I am your servant;
	yes, I am your servant, the son of your handmaid,
	and you have freed me from my bonds!
¹⁷I will offer you a sacrifice of thanksgiving
	and call on the name of the LORD.
¹⁸I will keep my promises to the LORD
	in the presence of all his people,
¹⁹in the house of the LORD,
	in the heart of Jerusalem.

Praise the LORD!

PSALM 117

¹Praise the LORD, all you nations.
	Praise him, all you people of the earth.

²For he loves us with unfailing love;
    the faithfulness of the LORD endures forever.

Praise the LORD!

PSALM 118

¹Give thanks to the LORD, for he is good!
    His faithful love endures forever.

²Let the congregation of Israel repeat:
    "His faithful love endures forever."
³Let Aaron's descendants, the priests, repeat:
    "His faithful love endures forever."
⁴Let all who fear the LORD repeat:
    "His faithful love endures forever."

⁵In my distress I prayed to the LORD,
    and the LORD answered me and rescued me.
⁶The LORD is for me, so I will not be afraid.
    What can mere mortals do to me?
⁷Yes, the LORD is for me; he will help me.
    I will look in triumph at those who hate me.
⁸It is better to trust the LORD
    than to put confidence in people.

⁹It is better to trust the LORD
>than to put confidence in princes.

¹⁰Though hostile nations surrounded me,
>I destroyed them all in the name of the LORD.
¹¹Yes, they surrounded and attacked me,
>but I destroyed them all in the name of the LORD.
¹²They swarmed around me like bees;
>they blazed against me like a roaring flame.
>But I destroyed them all in the name of the LORD.
¹³You did your best to kill me, O my enemy,
>but the LORD helped me.
¹⁴The LORD is my strength and my song;
>he has become my victory.
¹⁵Songs of joy and victory are sung in the camp of the
>godly.
>The strong right arm of the LORD has done glorious
>things!
¹⁶The strong right arm of the LORD is raised in triumph.
>The strong right arm of the LORD has done glorious
>things!
¹⁷I will not die, but I will live
>to tell what the LORD has done.
¹⁸The LORD has punished me severely,
>but he has not handed me over to death.

¹⁹Open for me the gates where the righteous enter,
and I will go in and thank the LORD.
²⁰Those gates lead to the presence of the LORD,
and the godly enter there.
²¹I thank you for answering my prayer
and saving me!

²²The stone rejected by the builders
has now become the cornerstone.
²³This is the LORD's doing,
and it is marvelous to see.
²⁴This is the day the LORD has made.
We will rejoice and be glad in it.
²⁵Please, LORD, please save us.
Please, LORD, please give us success.
²⁶Bless the one who comes in the name of the LORD.
We bless you from the house of the LORD.
²⁷The LORD is God, shining upon us.
Bring forward the sacrifice and put it on the altar.
²⁸You are my God, and I will praise you!
You are my God, and I will exalt you!

²⁹Give thanks to the LORD, for he is good!
His faithful love endures forever.

These are more proverbs of Solomon, collected by the advisers of King Hezekiah of Judah.

²It is God's privilege to conceal things and the king's privilege to discover them.

³No one can discover the height of heaven, the depth of the earth, or all that goes on in the king's mind!

⁴Remove the dross from silver, and the sterling will be ready for the silversmith. ⁵Remove the wicked from the king's court, and his reign will be made secure by justice.

⁶Don't demand an audience with the king or push for a place among the great. ⁷It is better to wait for an invitation than to be sent to the end of the line, publicly disgraced!

Just because you see something, ⁸don't be in a hurry to go to court. You might go down before your neighbors in shameful defeat. ⁹So discuss the matter with them privately. Don't tell anyone else, ¹⁰or others may accuse you of gossip. Then you will never regain your good reputation.

¹¹Timely advice is as lovely as golden apples in a silver basket.

¹²Valid criticism is as treasured by the one who heeds it as jewelry made from finest gold.

¹³Faithful messengers are as refreshing as snow in the heat of summer. They revive the spirit of their employer.

¹⁴A person who doesn't give a promised gift is like clouds and wind that don't bring rain.

¹⁵Patience can persuade a prince, and soft speech can crush strong opposition.

¹⁶Do you like honey? Don't eat too much of it, or it will make you sick!

¹⁷Don't visit your neighbors too often, or you will wear out your welcome.

¹⁸Telling lies about others is as harmful as hitting them with an ax, wounding them with a sword, or shooting them with a sharp arrow.

¹⁹Putting confidence in an unreliable person is like chewing with a toothache or walking on a broken foot.

²⁰Singing cheerful songs to a person whose heart is heavy is as bad as stealing someone's jacket in cold weather or rubbing salt in a wound.

²¹If your enemies are hungry, give them food to eat. If they are thirsty, give them water to drink. ²²You will heap burning coals on their heads, and the LORD will reward you.

²³As surely as a wind from the north brings rain, so a gossiping tongue causes anger!

24It is better to live alone in the corner of an attic than with a contentious wife in a lovely home.

25Good news from far away is like cold water to the thirsty.

26If the godly compromise with the wicked, it is like polluting a fountain or muddying a spring.

27Just as it is not good to eat too much honey, it is not good for people to think about all the honors they deserve.

28A person without self-control is as defenseless as a city with broken-down walls.

DAY TWENTY-SIX

PSALM 119

¹Happy are people of integrity,
    who follow the law of the LORD.
²Happy are those who obey his decrees
    and search for him with all their hearts.
³They do not compromise with evil,
    and they walk only in his paths.
⁴You have charged us
    to keep your commandments carefully.
⁵Oh, that my actions would consistently
    reflect your principles!
⁶Then I will not be disgraced
    when I compare my life with your commands.
⁷When I learn your righteous laws,
    I will thank you by living as I should!
⁸I will obey your principles.
    Please don't give up on me!

⁹How can a young person stay pure?

By obeying your word and following its rules.

¹⁰I have tried my best to find you—

don't let me wander from your commands.

¹¹I have hidden your word in my heart,

that I might not sin against you.

¹²Blessed are you, O LORD;

teach me your principles.

¹³I have recited aloud

all the laws you have given us.

¹⁴I have rejoiced in your decrees

as much as in riches.

¹⁵I will study your commandments

and reflect on your ways.

¹⁶I will delight in your principles

and not forget your word.

¹⁷Be good to your servant,

that I may live and obey your word.

¹⁸Open my eyes to see

the wonderful truths in your law.

¹⁹I am but a foreigner here on earth;

I need the guidance of your commands.

Don't hide them from me!

²⁰I am overwhelmed continually
    with a desire for your laws.
²¹You rebuke those cursed proud ones
    who wander from your commands.
²²Don't let them scorn and insult me,
    for I have obeyed your decrees.
²³Even princes sit and speak against me,
    but I will meditate on your principles.
²⁴Your decrees please me;
    they give me wise advice.

²⁵I lie in the dust, completely discouraged;
    revive me by your word.
²⁶I told you my plans, and you answered.
    Now teach me your principles.
²⁷Help me understand the meaning of your commandments,
    and I will meditate on your wonderful miracles.
²⁸I weep with grief;
    encourage me by your word.
²⁹Keep me from lying to myself;
    give me the privilege of knowing your law.
³⁰I have chosen to be faithful;
    I have determined to live by your laws.
³¹I cling to your decrees.
    LORD, don't let me be put to shame!

³²If you will help me,
   I will run to follow your commands.

³³Teach me, O LORD,
   to follow every one of your principles.
³⁴Give me understanding and I will obey your law;
   I will put it into practice with all my heart.
³⁵Make me walk along the path of your commands,
   for that is where my happiness is found.
³⁶Give me an eagerness for your decrees;
   do not inflict me with love for money!
³⁷Turn my eyes from worthless things,
   and give me life through your word.
³⁸Reassure me of your promise,
   which is for those who honor you.
³⁹Help me abandon my shameful ways;
   your laws are all I want in life.
⁴⁰I long to obey your commandments!
   Renew my life with your goodness.

⁴¹LORD, give to me your unfailing love,
   the salvation that you promised me.
⁴²Then I will have an answer for those who taunt me,
   for I trust in your word.
⁴³Do not snatch your word of truth from me,
   for my only hope is in your laws.

⁴⁴I will keep on obeying your law
    forever and forever.
⁴⁵I will walk in freedom,
    for I have devoted myself to your commandments.
⁴⁶I will speak to kings about your decrees,
    and I will not be ashamed.
⁴⁷How I delight in your commands!
    How I love them!
⁴⁸I honor and love your commands.
    I meditate on your principles.

⁴⁹Remember your promise to me,
    for it is my only hope.
⁵⁰Your promise revives me;
    it comforts me in all my troubles.
⁵¹The proud hold me in utter contempt,
    but I do not turn away from your law.
⁵²I meditate on your age-old laws;
    O LORD, they comfort me.
⁵³I am furious with the wicked,
    those who reject your law.
⁵⁴Your principles have been the music of my life
    throughout the years of my pilgrimage.
⁵⁵I reflect at night on who you are, O LORD,
    and I obey your law because of this.

⁵⁶This is my happy way of life:
    obeying your commandments.

⁵⁷LORD, you are mine!
    I promise to obey your words!
⁵⁸With all my heart I want your blessings.
    Be merciful just as you promised.
⁵⁹I pondered the direction of my life,
    and I turned to follow your statutes.
⁶⁰I will hurry, without lingering,
    to obey your commands.
⁶¹Evil people try to drag me into sin,
    but I am firmly anchored to your law.
⁶²At midnight I rise to thank you
    for your just laws.
⁶³Anyone who fears you is my friend—
    anyone who obeys your commandments.
⁶⁴O LORD, the earth is full of your unfailing love;
    teach me your principles.

⁶⁵You have done many good things for me, LORD,
    just as you promised.
⁶⁶I believe in your commands;
    now teach me good judgment and knowledge.
⁶⁷I used to wander off until you disciplined me;
    but now I closely follow your word.

⁶⁸You are good and do only good;
>   teach me your principles.
⁶⁹Arrogant people have made up lies about me,
>   but in truth I obey your commandments with all my
>   heart.
⁷⁰Their hearts are dull and stupid,
>   but I delight in your law.
⁷¹The suffering you sent was good for me,
>   for it taught me to pay attention to your principles.
⁷²Your law is more valuable to me
>   than millions in gold and silver!

⁷³You made me; you created me.
>   Now give me the sense to follow your commands.
⁷⁴May all who fear you find in me a cause for joy,
>   for I have put my hope in your word.
⁷⁵I know, O LORD, that your decisions are fair;
>   you disciplined me because I needed it.
⁷⁶Now let your unfailing love comfort me,
>   just as you promised me, your servant.
⁷⁷Surround me with your tender mercies so I may live,
>   for your law is my delight.
⁷⁸Bring disgrace upon the arrogant people who lied
>   about me;
>   meanwhile, I will concentrate on your commandments.

79Let me be reconciled

with all who fear you and know your decrees.
80May I be blameless in keeping your principles;

then I will never have to be ashamed.

81I faint with longing for your salvation;

but I have put my hope in your word.
82My eyes are straining to see your promises come true.

When will you comfort me?
83I am shriveled like a wineskin in the smoke, exhausted

with waiting.

But I cling to your principles and obey them.
84How long must I wait?

When will you punish those who persecute me?
85These arrogant people who hate your law

have dug deep pits for me to fall into.
86All your commands are trustworthy.

Protect me from those who hunt me down without cause.
87They almost finished me off,

but I refused to abandon your commandments.
88In your unfailing love, spare my life;

then I can continue to obey your decrees.

89Forever, O LORD,

your word stands firm in heaven.

⁹⁰Your faithfulness extends to every generation,
    as enduring as the earth you created.
⁹¹Your laws remain true today,
    for everything serves your plans.
⁹²If your law hadn't sustained me with joy,
    I would have died in my misery.
⁹³I will never forget your commandments,
    for you have used them to restore my joy and
        health.
⁹⁴I am yours; save me!
    For I have applied myself to obey your
        commandments.
⁹⁵Though the wicked hide along the way to kill me,
    I will quietly keep my mind on your decrees.
⁹⁶Even perfection has its limits,
    but your commands have no limit.

⁹⁷Oh, how I love your law!
    I think about it all day long.
⁹⁸Your commands make me wiser than my enemies,
    for your commands are my constant guide.
⁹⁹Yes, I have more insight than my teachers,
    for I am always thinking of your decrees.
¹⁰⁰I am even wiser than my elders,
    for I have kept your commandments.

¹⁰¹I have refused to walk on any path of evil,
  that I may remain obedient to your word.
¹⁰²I haven't turned away from your laws,
  for you have taught me well.
¹⁰³How sweet are your words to my taste;
  they are sweeter than honey.
¹⁰⁴Your commandments give me understanding;
  no wonder I hate every false way of life.

¹⁰⁵Your word is a lamp for my feet
  and a light for my path.
¹⁰⁶I've promised it once, and I'll promise again:
  I will obey your wonderful laws.
¹⁰⁷I have suffered much, O LORD;
  restore my life again, just as you promised.
¹⁰⁸LORD, accept my grateful thanks
  and teach me your laws.
¹⁰⁹My life constantly hangs in the balance,
  but I will not stop obeying your law.
¹¹⁰The wicked have set their traps for me along your path,
  but I will not turn from your commandments.
¹¹¹Your decrees are my treasure;
  they are truly my heart's delight.
¹¹²I am determined to keep your principles,
  even forever, to the very end.

[113]I hate those who are undecided about you,
   but my choice is clear—I love your law.
[114]You are my refuge and my shield;
   your word is my only source of hope.
[115]Get out of my life, you evil-minded people,
   for I intend to obey the commands of my God.
[116]LORD, sustain me as you promised, that I may live!
   Do not let my hope be crushed.
[117]Sustain me, and I will be saved;
   then I will meditate on your principles
      continually.
[118]But you have rejected all who stray from your
      principles.
   They are only fooling themselves.
[119]All the wicked of the earth are the scum you skim off;
   no wonder I love to obey your decrees!
[120]I tremble in fear of you;
   I fear your judgments.

[121]Don't leave me to the mercy of my enemies,
   for I have done what is just and right.
[122]Please guarantee a blessing for me.
   Don't let those who are arrogant oppress me!
[123]My eyes strain to see your deliverance,
   to see the truth of your promise fulfilled.

[124]I am your servant;

    deal with me in unfailing love,

    and teach me your principles.

[125]Give discernment to me, your servant;

    then I will understand your decrees.

[126]LORD, it is time for you to act,

    for these evil people have broken your law.

[127]Truly, I love your commands

    more than gold, even the finest gold.

[128]Truly, each of your commandments is right.

    That is why I hate every false way.

[129]Your decrees are wonderful.

    No wonder I obey them!

[130]As your words are taught, they give light;

    even the simple can understand them.

[131]I open my mouth, panting expectantly,

    longing for your commands.

[132]Come and show me your mercy,

    as you do for all who love your name.

[133]Guide my steps by your word,

    so I will not be overcome by any evil.

[134]Rescue me from the oppression of evil people;

    then I can obey your commandments.

¹³⁵Look down on me with love;
    teach me all your principles.
¹³⁶Rivers of tears gush from my eyes
    because people disobey your law.

¹³⁷O LORD, you are righteous,
    and your decisions are fair.
¹³⁸Your decrees are perfect;
    they are entirely worthy of our trust.
¹³⁹I am overwhelmed with rage,
    for my enemies have disregarded your words.
¹⁴⁰Your promises have been thoroughly tested;
    that is why I love them so much.
¹⁴¹I am insignificant and despised,
    but I don't forget your commandments.
¹⁴²Your justice is eternal,
    and your law is perfectly true.
¹⁴³As pressure and stress bear down on me,
    I find joy in your commands.
¹⁴⁴Your decrees are always fair;
    help me to understand them, that I may live.

¹⁴⁵I pray with all my heart; answer me, LORD!
    I will obey your principles.
¹⁴⁶I cry out to you; save me,
    that I may obey your decrees.

¹⁴⁷I rise early, before the sun is up;
   I cry out for help and put my hope in your words.
¹⁴⁸I stay awake through the night,
   thinking about your promise.
¹⁴⁹In your faithful love, O LORD, hear my cry;
   in your justice, save my life.
¹⁵⁰Those lawless people are coming near to attack me;
   they live far from your law.
¹⁵¹But you are near, O LORD,
   and all your commands are true.
¹⁵²I have known from my earliest days
   that your decrees never change.

¹⁵³Look down upon my sorrows and rescue me,
   for I have not forgotten your law.
¹⁵⁴Argue my case; take my side!
   Protect my life as you promised.
¹⁵⁵The wicked are far from salvation,
   for they do not bother with your principles.
¹⁵⁶LORD, how great is your mercy;
   in your justice, give me back my life.
¹⁵⁷Many persecute and trouble me,
   yet I have not swerved from your decrees.
¹⁵⁸I hate these traitors
   because they care nothing for your word.

159See how I love your commandments, LORD.
  Give back my life because of your unfailing love.
160All your words are true;
  all your just laws will stand forever.

161Powerful people harass me without cause,
  but my heart trembles only at your word.
162I rejoice in your word
  like one who finds a great treasure.
163I hate and abhor all falsehood,
  but I love your law.
164I will praise you seven times a day
  because all your laws are just.
165Those who love your law have great peace
  and do not stumble.
166I long for your salvation, LORD,
  so I have obeyed your commands.
167I have obeyed your decrees,
  and I love them very much.
168Yes, I obey your commandments and decrees,
  because you know everything I do.

169O LORD, listen to my cry;
  give me the discerning mind you promised.
170Listen to my prayer;
  rescue me as you promised.

¹⁷¹Let my lips burst forth with praise,
>   for you have taught me your principles.
¹⁷²Let my tongue sing about your word,
>   for all your commands are right.
¹⁷³Stand ready to help me,
>   for I have chosen to follow your commandments.
¹⁷⁴O LORD, I have longed for your salvation,
>   and your law is my delight.
¹⁷⁵Let me live so I can praise you,
>   and may your laws sustain me.
¹⁷⁶I have wandered away like a lost sheep;
>   come and find me,
>   for I have not forgotten your commands.

PROVERBS 26

Honor doesn't go with fools any more than snow with summer or rain with harvest.

²Like a fluttering sparrow or a darting swallow, an unfair curse will not land on its intended victim.

³Guide a horse with a whip, a donkey with a bridle, and a fool with a rod to his back!

⁴When arguing with fools, don't answer their foolish arguments, or you will become as foolish as they are.

⁵When arguing with fools, be sure to answer their

foolish arguments, or they will become wise in their own estimation.

⁶Trusting a fool to convey a message is as foolish as cutting off one's feet or drinking poison!

⁷In the mouth of a fool, a proverb becomes as limp as a paralyzed leg.

⁸Honoring a fool is as foolish as tying a stone to a slingshot.

⁹A proverb in a fool's mouth is as dangerous as a thornbush brandished by a drunkard.

¹⁰An employer who hires a fool or a bystander is like an archer who shoots recklessly.

¹¹As a dog returns to its vomit, so a fool repeats his folly.

¹²There is more hope for fools than for people who think they are wise.

¹³The lazy person is full of excuses, saying, "I can't go outside because there might be a lion on the road! Yes, I'm sure there's a lion out there!"

¹⁴As a door turns back and forth on its hinges, so the lazy person turns over in bed.

¹⁵Some people are so lazy that they won't lift a finger to feed themselves.

¹⁶Lazy people consider themselves smarter than seven wise counselors.

¹⁷Yanking a dog's ears is as foolish as interfering in someone else's argument.

¹⁸Just as damaging as a mad man shooting a lethal weapon ¹⁹is someone who lies to a friend and then says, "I was only joking."

²⁰Fire goes out for lack of fuel, and quarrels disappear when gossip stops.

²¹A quarrelsome person starts fights as easily as hot embers light charcoal or fire lights wood.

²²What dainty morsels rumors are—but they sink deep into one's heart.

²³Smooth words may hide a wicked heart, just as a pretty glaze covers a common clay pot.

²⁴People with hate in their hearts may sound pleasant enough, but don't believe them. ²⁵Though they pretend to be kind, their hearts are full of all kinds of evil. ²⁶While their hatred may be concealed by trickery, it will finally come to light for all to see.

²⁷If you set a trap for others, you will get caught in it yourself. If you roll a boulder down on others, it will roll back and crush you.

²⁸A lying tongue hates its victims, and flattery causes ruin.

DAY TWENTY-SEVEN

PSALM 120

A song for the ascent to Jerusalem.

¹I took my troubles to the LORD;
   I cried out to him, and he answered my prayer.
²Rescue me, O LORD, from liars
   and from all deceitful people.
³O deceptive tongue, what will God do to you?
   How will he increase your punishment?
⁴You will be pierced with sharp arrows
   and burned with glowing coals.

⁵How I suffer among these scoundrels of Meshech!
   It pains me to live with these people from Kedar!
⁶I am tired of living here
   among people who hate peace.
⁷As for me, I am for peace;
   but when I speak, they are for war!

PSALM 121

A song for the ascent to Jerusalem.

¹I look up to the mountains—
   does my help come from there?
²My help comes from the LORD,
   who made the heavens and the earth!

³He will not let you stumble and fall;
   the one who watches over you will not sleep.
⁴Indeed, he who watches over Israel
   never tires and never sleeps.

⁵The LORD himself watches over you!
   The LORD stands beside you as your protective shade.
⁶The sun will not hurt you by day,
   nor the moon at night.
⁷The LORD keeps you from all evil
   and preserves your life.
⁸The LORD keeps watch over you as you come and go,
   both now and forever.

PSALM 122

A song for the ascent to Jerusalem. A psalm of David.

¹I was glad when they said to me,
    "Let us go to the house of the LORD."
²And now we are standing here
    inside your gates, O Jerusalem.
³Jerusalem is a well-built city,
    knit together as a single unit.
⁴All the people of Israel—the LORD's people—
    make their pilgrimage here.
They come to give thanks to the name of the LORD
    as the law requires.
⁵Here stand the thrones where judgment is given,
    the thrones of the dynasty of David.

⁶Pray for the peace of Jerusalem.
    May all who love this city prosper.
⁷O Jerusalem, may there be peace within your walls
    and prosperity in your palaces.
⁸For the sake of my family and friends, I will say,
    "Peace be with you."
⁹For the sake of the house of the LORD our God,
    I will seek what is best for you, O Jerusalem.

PSALM 123

A song for the ascent to Jerusalem.

¹I lift my eyes to you,
    O God, enthroned in heaven.
²We look to the LORD our God for his mercy,
    just as servants keep their eyes on their master,
    as a slave girl watches her mistress for the slightest
        signal.

³Have mercy on us, LORD, have mercy,
    for we have had our fill of contempt.
⁴We have had our fill of the scoffing of the proud
    and the contempt of the arrogant.

PSALM 124

A song for the ascent to Jerusalem. A psalm of David.

¹If the LORD had not been on our side—
    let Israel now say—
²if the LORD had not been on our side
    when people rose up against us,
³they would have swallowed us alive
    because of their burning anger against us.
⁴The waters would have engulfed us;
    a torrent would have overwhelmed us.

⁵Yes, the raging waters of their fury
   would have overwhelmed our very lives.

⁶Blessed be the LORD,
   who did not let their teeth tear us apart!
⁷We escaped like a bird from a hunter's trap.
   The trap is broken, and we are free!
⁸Our help is from the LORD,
   who made the heavens and the earth.

PSALM 125

A song for the ascent to Jerusalem.

¹Those who trust in the LORD are as secure as Mount Zion;
   they will not be defeated but will endure forever.
²Just as the mountains surround and protect Jerusalem,
   so the LORD surrounds and protects his people, both
      now and forever.
³The wicked will not rule the godly,
   for then the godly might be forced to do wrong.
⁴O LORD, do good to those who are good,
   whose hearts are in tune with you.
⁵But banish those who turn to crooked ways, O LORD.
   Take them away with those who do evil.
   And let Israel have quietness and peace.

PSALM 126

A song for the ascent to Jerusalem.

¹When the LORD restored his exiles to Jerusalem,
   it was like a dream!
²We were filled with laughter,
   and we sang for joy.
And the other nations said,
   "What amazing things the LORD has done for
      them."
³Yes, the LORD has done amazing things for us!
   What joy!

⁴Restore our fortunes, LORD,
   as streams renew the desert.
⁵Those who plant in tears
   will harvest with shouts of joy.
⁶They weep as they go to plant their seed,
   but they sing as they return with the harvest.

PSALM 127

A song for the ascent to Jerusalem. A psalm of Solomon.

¹Unless the LORD builds a house,
   the work of the builders is useless.

Unless the LORD protects a city,
    guarding it with sentries will do no good.
²It is useless for you to work so hard
    from early morning until late at night,
anxiously working for food to eat;
    for God gives rest to his loved ones.

³Children are a gift from the LORD;
    they are a reward from him.
⁴Children born to a young man
    are like sharp arrows in a warrior's hands.
⁵How happy is the man whose quiver is full of them!
    He will not be put to shame when he confronts his
        accusers at the city gates.

PSALM 128

A song for the ascent to Jerusalem.

¹How happy are those who fear the LORD—
    all who follow his ways!
²You will enjoy the fruit of your labor.
    How happy you will be! How rich your life!
³Your wife will be like a fruitful vine,
    flourishing within your home.
And look at all those children!

There they sit around your table
    as vigorous and healthy as young olive trees.
⁴That is the LORD's reward
    for those who fear him.

⁵May the LORD continually bless you from Zion.
    May you see Jerusalem prosper as long as you live.
⁶May you live to enjoy your grandchildren.
    And may Israel have quietness and peace.

PSALM 129

A song for the ascent to Jerusalem.

¹From my earliest youth my enemies have persecuted
        me—
    let Israel now say—
²from my earliest youth my enemies have persecuted me,
    but they have never been able to finish me off.
³My back is covered with cuts,
    as if a farmer had plowed long furrows.
⁴But the LORD is good;
    he has cut the cords used by the ungodly to bind me.

⁵May all who hate Jerusalem
    be turned back in shameful defeat.

⁶May they be as useless as grass on a rooftop,
   turning yellow when only half grown,
⁷   ignored by the harvester,
   despised by the binder.
⁸And may those who pass by refuse to give them this
      blessing:
   "The LORD's blessings be upon you;
   we bless you in the LORD's name."

PROVERBS 27

Don't brag about tomorrow, since you don't know what
the day will bring.

²Don't praise yourself; let others do it!

³A stone is heavy and sand is weighty, but the resent-
ment caused by a fool is heavier than both.

⁴Anger is cruel, and wrath is like a flood, but who can
survive the destructiveness of jealousy?

⁵An open rebuke is better than hidden love!

⁶Wounds from a friend are better than many kisses
from an enemy.

⁷Honey seems tasteless to a person who is full, but
even bitter food tastes sweet to the hungry.

⁸A person who strays from home is like a bird that
strays from its nest.

⁹The heartfelt counsel of a friend is as sweet as perfume and incense.

¹⁰Never abandon a friend—either yours or your father's. Then in your time of need, you won't have to ask your relatives for assistance. It is better to go to a neighbor than to a relative who lives far away.

¹¹My child, how happy I will be if you turn out to be wise! Then I will be able to answer my critics.

¹²A prudent person foresees the danger ahead and takes precautions. The simpleton goes blindly on and suffers the consequences.

¹³Be sure to get collateral from anyone who guarantees the debt of a stranger. Get a deposit if someone guarantees the debt of an adulterous woman.

¹⁴If you shout a pleasant greeting to your neighbor too early in the morning, it will be counted as a curse!

¹⁵A nagging wife is as annoying as the constant dripping on a rainy day. ¹⁶Trying to stop her complaints is like trying to stop the wind or hold something with greased hands.

¹⁷As iron sharpens iron, a friend sharpens a friend.

¹⁸Workers who tend a fig tree are allowed to eat its fruit. In the same way, workers who protect their employer's interests will be rewarded.

¹⁹As a face is reflected in water, so the heart reflects the person.

²⁰Just as Death and Destruction are never satisfied, so human desire is never satisfied.

²¹Fire tests the purity of silver and gold, but a person is tested by being praised.

²²You cannot separate fools from their foolishness, even though you grind them like grain with mortar and pestle.

²³Know the state of your flocks, and put your heart into caring for your herds, ²⁴for riches don't last forever, and the crown might not be secure for the next generation. ²⁵After the hay is harvested, the new crop appears, and the mountain grasses are gathered in, ²⁶your sheep will provide wool for clothing, and your goats will be sold for the price of a field. ²⁷And you will have enough goats' milk for you, your family, and your servants.

DAY TWENTY-EIGHT

PSALM 130

A song for the ascent to Jerusalem.

¹From the depths of despair, O LORD,
    I call for your help.
²Hear my cry, O Lord.
    Pay attention to my prayer.

³LORD, if you kept a record of our sins,
    who, O Lord, could ever survive?
⁴But you offer forgiveness,
    that we might learn to fear you.

⁵I am counting on the LORD;
    yes, I am counting on him.
    I have put my hope in his word.
⁶I long for the Lord
    more than sentries long for the dawn,
    yes, more than sentries long for the dawn.

⁷O Israel, hope in the LORD;
 for with the LORD there is unfailing love
 and an overflowing supply of salvation.
⁸He himself will free Israel
 from every kind of sin.

PSALM 131

A song for the ascent to Jerusalem. A psalm of David.

¹LORD, my heart is not proud;
 my eyes are not haughty.
I don't concern myself with matters too great
 or awesome for me.
²But I have stilled and quieted myself,
 just as a small child is quiet with its mother.
 Yes, like a small child is my soul within me.

³O Israel, put your hope in the LORD—
 now and always.

PSALM 132

A song for the ascent to Jerusalem.

¹LORD, remember David
 and all that he suffered.

²He took an oath before the LORD.

He vowed to the Mighty One of Israel,

³"I will not go home;

I will not let myself rest.

⁴I will not let my eyes sleep

nor close my eyelids in slumber

5   until I find a place to build a house for the LORD,

a sanctuary for the Mighty One of Israel."

⁶We heard that the Ark was in Ephrathah;

then we found it in the distant countryside of Jaar.

⁷Let us go to the dwelling place of the LORD;

let us bow low before him.

⁸Arise, O LORD, and enter your sanctuary,

along with the Ark, the symbol of your power.

⁹Your priests will be agents of salvation;

may your loyal servants sing for joy.

¹⁰For the sake of your servant David,

do not reject the king you chose for your people.

¹¹The LORD swore to David

a promise he will never take back:

"I will place one of your descendants on your throne.

¹²If your descendants obey the terms of my covenant

and follow the decrees that I teach them,

then your royal line will never end."

¹³For the Lord has chosen Jerusalem;
>	he has desired it as his home.
¹⁴"This is my home where I will live forever," he said.
>	"I will live here, for this is the place I desired.
¹⁵I will make this city prosperous
>	and satisfy its poor with food.
¹⁶I will make its priests the agents of salvation;
>	its godly people will sing for joy.
¹⁷Here I will increase the power of David;
>	my anointed one will be a light for my people.
¹⁸I will clothe his enemies with shame,
>	but he will be a glorious king."

PSALM 133

A song for the ascent to Jerusalem. A psalm of David.

¹How wonderful it is, how pleasant,
>	when brothers live together in harmony!
²For harmony is as precious as the fragrant anointing oil
>	that was poured over Aaron's head,
>	that ran down his beard
>	and onto the border of his robe.
³Harmony is as refreshing as the dew from Mount Hermon
>	that falls on the mountains of Zion.

And the LORD has pronounced his blessing,
    even life forevermore.

PSALM 134

A song for the ascent to Jerusalem.

¹Oh, bless the LORD, all you servants of the LORD,
    you who serve as night watchmen in the house of the
        LORD.
²Lift your hands in holiness,
    and bless the LORD.

³May the LORD, who made heaven and earth,
    bless you from Jerusalem.

PROVERBS 28

The wicked run away when no one is chasing them, but
the godly are as bold as lions.

²When there is moral rot within a nation, its govern-
ment topples easily. But with wise and knowledgeable
leaders, there is stability.

³A poor person who oppresses the poor is like a
pounding rain that destroys the crops.

⁴To reject the law is to praise the wicked; to obey the
law is to fight them.

⁵Evil people don't understand justice, but those who follow the LORD understand completely.

⁶It is better to be poor and honest than rich and crooked.

⁷Young people who obey the law are wise; those who seek out worthless companions bring shame to their parents.

⁸A person who makes money by charging interest will lose it. It will end up in the hands of someone who is kind to the poor.

⁹The prayers of a person who ignores the law are despised.

¹⁰Those who lead the upright into sin will fall into their own trap, but the honest will inherit good things.

¹¹Rich people picture themselves as wise, but their real poverty is evident to the poor.

¹²When the godly succeed, everyone is glad. When the wicked take charge, people go into hiding.

¹³People who cover over their sins will not prosper. But if they confess and forsake them, they will receive mercy.

¹⁴Blessed are those who have a tender conscience, but the stubborn are headed for serious trouble.

¹⁵A wicked ruler is as dangerous to the poor as a lion or bear attacking them.

¹⁶Only a stupid prince will oppress his people, but a king will have a long reign if he hates dishonesty and bribes.

¹⁷A murderer's tormented conscience will drive him into the grave. Don't protect him!

¹⁸The honest will be rescued from harm, but those who are crooked will be destroyed.

¹⁹Hard workers have plenty of food; playing around brings poverty.

²⁰The trustworthy will get a rich reward. But the person who wants to get rich quick will only get into trouble.

²¹Showing partiality is never good, yet some will do wrong for something as small as a piece of bread.

²²A greedy person tries to get rich quick, but it only leads to poverty.

²³In the end, people appreciate frankness more than flattery.

²⁴Robbing your parents and then saying, "What's wrong with that?" is as serious as committing murder.

²⁵Greed causes fighting; trusting the LORD leads to prosperity.

²⁶Trusting oneself is foolish, but those who walk in wisdom are safe.

²⁷Whoever gives to the poor will lack nothing. But a curse will come upon those who close their eyes to poverty.

²⁸When the wicked take charge, people hide. When the wicked meet disaster, the godly multiply.

DAY TWENTY-NINE

PSALM 135

¹Praise the LORD!

Praise the name of the LORD!
Praise him, you who serve the LORD,
　² 　you who serve in the house of the LORD,
　　in the courts of the house of our God.
³Praise the LORD, for the LORD is good;
　　celebrate his wonderful name with music.
⁴For the LORD has chosen Jacob for himself,
　　Israel for his own special treasure.

⁵I know the greatness of the LORD—
　　that our Lord is greater than any other god.
⁶The LORD does whatever pleases him
　　throughout all heaven and earth,
　　and on the seas and in their depths.
⁷He causes the clouds to rise over the earth.
　　He sends the lightning with the rain
　　and releases the wind from his storehouses.

⁸He destroyed the firstborn in each Egyptian home,
    both people and animals.
⁹He performed miraculous signs and wonders in Egypt;
    Pharaoh and all his people watched.
¹⁰He struck down great nations
    and slaughtered mighty kings—
¹¹   Sihon king of the Amorites,
    Og king of Bashan,
    and all the kings of Canaan.
¹²He gave their land as an inheritance,
    a special possession to his people Israel.
¹³Your name, O LORD, endures forever;
    your fame, O LORD, is known to every generation.
¹⁴For the LORD will vindicate his people
    and have compassion on his servants.

¹⁵Their idols are merely things of silver and gold,
    shaped by human hands.
¹⁶They cannot talk, though they have mouths,
    or see, though they have eyes!
¹⁷They cannot hear with their ears
    or smell with their noses.
¹⁸And those who make them are just like them,
    as are all who trust in them.

¹⁹O Israel, praise the LORD!

O priests of Aaron, praise the LORD!
²⁰O Levites, praise the LORD!

All you who fear the LORD, praise the LORD!
²¹The LORD be praised from Zion,

for he lives here in Jerusalem.

Praise the LORD!

PSALM 136

¹Give thanks to the LORD, for he is good!

His faithful love endures forever.
²Give thanks to the God of gods.

His faithful love endures forever.
³Give thanks to the Lord of lords.

His faithful love endures forever.

⁴Give thanks to him who alone does mighty miracles.

His faithful love endures forever.
⁵Give thanks to him who made the heavens so skillfully.

His faithful love endures forever.
⁶Give thanks to him who placed the earth on the water.

His faithful love endures forever.
⁷Give thanks to him who made the heavenly lights—

His faithful love endures forever.

⁸   the sun to rule the day,

His faithful love endures forever.

⁹   and the moon and stars to rule the night.

His faithful love endures forever.

¹⁰Give thanks to him who killed the firstborn of Egypt.

His faithful love endures forever.

¹¹He brought Israel out of Egypt.

His faithful love endures forever.

¹²He acted with a strong hand and powerful arm.

His faithful love endures forever.

¹³Give thanks to him who parted the Red Sea.

His faithful love endures forever.

¹⁴He led Israel safely through,

His faithful love endures forever.

¹⁵   but he hurled Pharaoh and his army into the sea.

His faithful love endures forever.

¹⁶Give thanks to him who led his people through the wilderness.

His faithful love endures forever.

¹⁷Give thanks to him who struck down mighty kings.

His faithful love endures forever.

¹⁸He killed powerful kings—

His faithful love endures forever.

¹⁹   Sihon king of the Amorites,

His faithful love endures forever.

²⁰   and Og king of Bashan.

His faithful love endures forever.

²¹God gave the land of these kings as an inheritance—

His faithful love endures forever.

²²   a special possession to his servant Israel.

His faithful love endures forever.

²³He remembered our utter weakness.

His faithful love endures forever.

²⁴He saved us from our enemies.

His faithful love endures forever.

²⁵He gives food to every living thing.

His faithful love endures forever.

²⁶Give thanks to the God of heaven.

His faithful love endures forever.

PSALM 137

¹Beside the rivers of Babylon, we sat and wept
  as we thought of Jerusalem.
²We put away our lyres,
  hanging them on the branches of the willow trees.
³For there our captors demanded a song of us.
  Our tormentors requested a joyful hymn:
  "Sing us one of those songs of Jerusalem!"

⁴But how can we sing the songs of the LORD
    while in a foreign land?

⁵If I forget you, O Jerusalem,
    let my right hand forget its skill upon the harp.
⁶May my tongue stick to the roof of my mouth
    if I fail to remember you,
    if I don't make Jerusalem my highest joy.

⁷O LORD, remember what the Edomites did
    on the day the armies of Babylon captured Jerusalem.
"Destroy it!" they yelled.
    "Level it to the ground!"
⁸O Babylon, you will be destroyed.
    Happy is the one who pays you back
    for what you have done to us.
⁹Happy is the one who takes your babies
    and smashes them against the rocks!

PSALM 138

A psalm of David.

¹I give you thanks, O LORD, with all my heart;
    I will sing your praises before the gods.
²I bow before your holy Temple as I worship.

I will give thanks to your name
  for your unfailing love and faithfulness,
because your promises are backed
  by all the honor of your name.
  ³When I pray, you answer me;
    you encourage me by giving me the strength I
      need.

⁴Every king in all the earth will give you thanks,
    O LORD,
  for all of them will hear your words.
⁵Yes, they will sing about the LORD's ways,
  for the glory of the LORD is very great.
⁶Though the LORD is great, he cares for the humble,
  but he keeps his distance from the proud.

⁷Though I am surrounded by troubles,
  you will preserve me against the anger of my
    enemies.
You will clench your fist against my angry enemies!
  Your power will save me.
⁸The LORD will work out his plans for my life—
  for your faithful love, O LORD, endures forever.
  Don't abandon me, for you made me.

PSALM 139

For the choir director: A psalm of David.

¹O LORD, you have examined my heart
   and know everything about me.
²You know when I sit down or stand up.
   You know my every thought when far away.
³You chart the path ahead of me
   and tell me where to stop and rest.
   Every moment you know where I am.
⁴You know what I am going to say
   even before I say it, LORD.
⁵You both precede and follow me.
   You place your hand of blessing on my head.
⁶Such knowledge is too wonderful for me,
   too great for me to know!

⁷I can never escape from your spirit!
   I can never get away from your presence!
⁸If I go up to heaven, you are there;
   if I go down to the place of the dead, you are there.
⁹If I ride the wings of the morning,
   if I dwell by the farthest oceans,
¹⁰even there your hand will guide me,
   and your strength will support me.

¹¹I could ask the darkness to hide me
    and the light around me to become night—
¹²   but even in darkness I cannot hide from you.
To you the night shines as bright as day.
    Darkness and light are both alike to you.

¹³You made all the delicate, inner parts of my body
    and knit me together in my mother's womb.
¹⁴Thank you for making me so wonderfully complex!
    Your workmanship is marvelous—and how well I
        know it.
¹⁵You watched me as I was being formed in utter
        seclusion,
    as I was woven together in the dark of the womb.
¹⁶You saw me before I was born.
    Every day of my life was recorded in your book.
Every moment was laid out
    before a single day had passed.

¹⁷How precious are your thoughts about me, O God!
    They are innumerable!
¹⁸I can't even count them;
    they outnumber the grains of sand!
And when I wake up in the morning,
    you are still with me!

¹⁹O God, if only you would destroy the wicked!
   Get out of my life, you murderers!
²⁰They blaspheme you;
   your enemies take your name in vain.
²¹O LORD, shouldn't I hate those who hate you?
   Shouldn't I despise those who resist you?
²²Yes, I hate them with complete hatred,
   for your enemies are my enemies.

²³Search me, O God, and know my heart;
   test me and know my thoughts.
²⁴Point out anything in me that offends you,
   and lead me along the path of everlasting life.

PROVERBS 29

Whoever stubbornly refuses to accept criticism will suddenly be broken beyond repair.

²When the godly are in authority, the people rejoice. But when the wicked are in power, they groan.

³The man who loves wisdom brings joy to his father, but if he hangs around with prostitutes, his wealth is wasted.

⁴A just king gives stability to his nation, but one who demands bribes destroys it.

⁵To flatter people is to lay a trap for their feet.

⁶Evil people are trapped by sin, but the righteous escape, shouting for joy.

⁷The godly know the rights of the poor; the wicked don't care to know.

⁸Mockers can get a whole town agitated, but those who are wise will calm anger.

⁹If a wise person takes a fool to court, there will be ranting and ridicule but no satisfaction.

¹⁰The bloodthirsty hate the honest, but the upright seek out the honest.

¹¹A fool gives full vent to anger, but a wise person quietly holds it back.

¹²If a ruler honors liars, all his advisers will be wicked.

¹³The poor and the oppressor have this in common— the LORD gives light to the eyes of both.

¹⁴A king who is fair to the poor will have a long reign.

¹⁵To discipline and reprimand a child produces wisdom, but a mother is disgraced by an undisciplined child.

¹⁶When the wicked are in authority, sin increases. But the godly will live to see the tyrant's downfall.

¹⁷Discipline your children, and they will give you happiness and peace of mind.

¹⁸When people do not accept divine guidance, they run wild. But whoever obeys the law is happy.

¹⁹For a servant, mere words are not enough—discipline is needed. For the words may be understood, but they are not heeded.

²⁰There is more hope for a fool than for someone who speaks without thinking.

²¹A servant who is pampered from childhood will later become a rebel.

²²A hot-tempered person starts fights and gets into all kinds of sin.

²³Pride ends in humiliation, while humility brings honor.

²⁴If you assist a thief, you are only hurting yourself. You will be punished if you report the crime, but you will be cursed if you don't.

²⁵Fearing people is a dangerous trap, but to trust the LORD means safety.

²⁶Many seek the ruler's favor, but justice comes from the LORD.

²⁷The godly despise the wicked; the wicked despise the godly.

DAY THIRTY

PSALM 140

For the choir director: A psalm of David.

¹O LORD, rescue me from evil people.
  Preserve me from those who are violent,
²those who plot evil in their hearts
  and stir up trouble all day long.
³Their tongues sting like a snake;
  the poison of a viper drips from their lips.   *Interlude*

⁴O LORD, keep me out of the hands of the wicked.
  Preserve me from those who are violent,
  for they are plotting against me.
⁵The proud have set a trap to catch me;
  they have stretched out a net;
  they have placed traps all along the way.   *Interlude*

⁶I said to the LORD, "You are my God!"
  Listen, O LORD, to my cries for mercy!

⁷O Sovereign LORD, my strong savior,
   you protected me on the day of battle.
⁸LORD, do not give in to their evil desires.
   Do not let their evil schemes succeed, O God.

Interlude

⁹Let my enemies be destroyed
   by the very evil they have planned for me.
¹⁰Let burning coals fall down on their heads,
   or throw them into the fire,
   or into deep pits from which they can't escape.
¹¹Don't let liars prosper here in our land.
   Cause disaster to fall with great force on the violent.

¹²But I know the LORD will surely help those they
         persecute;
   he will maintain the rights of the poor.
¹³Surely the godly are praising your name,
   for they will live in your presence.

PSALM 141

A psalm of David.

¹O LORD, I am calling to you. Please hurry!
   Listen when I cry to you for help!

²Accept my prayer as incense offered to you,
and my upraised hands as an evening offering.

³Take control of what I say, O LORD,
and keep my lips sealed.
⁴Don't let me lust for evil things;
don't let me participate in acts of wickedness.
Don't let me share in the delicacies
of those who do evil.

⁵Let the godly strike me!
It will be a kindness!
If they reprove me, it is soothing medicine.
Don't let me refuse it.

But I am in constant prayer
against the wicked and their deeds.
⁶When their leaders are thrown down from a cliff,
they will listen to my words and find them pleasing.
⁷Even as a farmer breaks up the soil and brings up rocks,
so the bones of the wicked will be scattered without a
decent burial.

⁸I look to you for help, O Sovereign LORD.
You are my refuge; don't let them kill me.
⁹Keep me out of the traps they have set for me,
out of the snares of those who do evil.

¹⁰Let the wicked fall into their own snares,
　　but let me escape.

PSALM 142

A psalm of David, regarding his experience in the cave. A prayer.

¹I cry out to the LORD;
　　I plead for the LORD's mercy.
²I pour out my complaints before him
　　and tell him all my troubles.
³For I am overwhelmed,
　　and you alone know the way I should turn.
Wherever I go,
　　my enemies have set traps for me.
⁴I look for someone to come and help me,
　　but no one gives me a passing thought!
No one will help me;
　　no one cares a bit what happens to me.
⁵Then I pray to you, O LORD.
　　I say, "You are my place of refuge.
　　You are all I really want in life.
⁶Hear my cry,
　　for I am very low.
Rescue me from my persecutors,
　　for they are too strong for me.

⁷Bring me out of prison
    so I can thank you.
The godly will crowd around me,
    for you treat me kindly."

PSALM 143

A psalm of David.

¹Hear my prayer, O L<small>ORD</small>;
    listen to my plea!
    Answer me because you are faithful and righteous.
²Don't bring your servant to trial!
    Compared to you, no one is perfect.
³My enemy has chased me.
    He has knocked me to the ground.
    He forces me to live in darkness like those in the
        grave.
⁴I am losing all hope;
    I am paralyzed with fear.
⁵I remember the days of old.
    I ponder all your great works.
    I think about what you have done.
⁶I reach out for you.
    I thirst for you as parched land thirsts for rain.   *Interlude*

7Come quickly, LORD, and answer me,
  for my depression deepens.
Don't turn away from me,
  or I will die.
8Let me hear of your unfailing love to me in the morning,
  for I am trusting you.
Show me where to walk,
  for I have come to you in prayer.
9Save me from my enemies, LORD;
  I run to you to hide me.
10Teach me to do your will,
  for you are my God.
May your gracious Spirit lead me forward
  on a firm footing.
11For the glory of your name, O LORD, save me.
  In your righteousness, bring me out of this distress.
12In your unfailing love, cut off all my enemies
  and destroy all my foes,
  for I am your servant.

PSALM 144

A psalm of David.

1Bless the LORD, who is my rock.

He gives me strength for war
and skill for battle.
²He is my loving ally and my fortress,
my tower of safety, my deliverer.
He stands before me as a shield, and I take refuge in him.
He subdues the nations under me.

³O LORD, what are mortals that you should notice us,
mere humans that you should care for us?
⁴For we are like a breath of air;
our days are like a passing shadow.

⁵Bend down the heavens, LORD, and come down.
Touch the mountains so they billow smoke.
⁶Release your lightning bolts and scatter your enemies!
Release your arrows and confuse them!
⁷Reach down from heaven and rescue me;
deliver me from deep waters,
from the power of my enemies.
⁸Their mouths are full of lies;
they swear to tell the truth, but they lie.

⁹I will sing a new song to you, O God!
I will sing your praises with a ten-stringed harp.
¹⁰For you grant victory to kings!
You are the one who rescued your servant David.

[11]Save me from the fatal sword!

   Rescue me from the power of my enemies.

Their mouths are full of lies;

   they swear to tell the truth, but they lie.

[12]May our sons flourish in their youth

   like well-nurtured plants.

May our daughters be like graceful pillars,

   carved to beautify a palace.

[13]May our farms be filled

   with crops of every kind.

May the flocks in our fields multiply by the thousands,

   even tens of thousands,

[14]   and may our oxen be loaded down with produce.

May there be no breached walls, no forced exile,

   no cries of distress in our squares.

[15]Yes, happy are those who have it like this!

   Happy indeed are those whose God is the LORD.

PROVERBS 30

The message of Agur son of Jakeh. An oracle.

   I am weary, O God; I am weary and worn out,
O God. [2]I am too ignorant to be human, and I lack
common sense. [3]I have not mastered human wisdom, nor
do I know the Holy One.

⁴Who but God goes up to heaven and comes back down? Who holds the wind in his fists? Who wraps up the oceans in his cloak? Who has created the whole wide world? What is his name—and his son's name? Tell me if you know!

⁵Every word of God proves true. He defends all who come to him for protection. ⁶Do not add to his words, or he may rebuke you, and you will be found a liar. ⁷O God, I beg two favors from you before I die. ⁸First, help me never to tell a lie. Second, give me neither poverty nor riches! Give me just enough to satisfy my needs. ⁹For if I grow rich, I may deny you and say, "Who is the LORD?" And if I am too poor, I may steal and thus insult God's holy name.

¹⁰Never slander a person to his employer. If you do, the person will curse you, and you will pay for it.

¹¹Some people curse their father and do not thank their mother. ¹²They feel pure, but they are filthy and unwashed. ¹³They are proud beyond description and disdainful. ¹⁴They devour the poor with teeth as sharp as swords or knives. They destroy the needy from the face of the earth.

¹⁵The leech has two suckers that cry out, "More, more!" There are three other things—no, four!—that are never satisfied:

¹⁶ the grave,
   the barren womb,
   the thirsty desert,
   the blazing fire.

¹⁷The eye that mocks a father and despises a mother will be plucked out by ravens of the valley and eaten by vultures.

¹⁸There are three things that amaze me—no, four things I do not understand:
¹⁹ how an eagle glides through the sky,
   how a snake slithers on a rock,
   how a ship navigates the ocean,
   how a man loves a woman.
²⁰Equally amazing is how an adulterous woman can satisfy her sexual appetite, shrug her shoulders, and then say, "What's wrong with that?"

²¹There are three things that make the earth tremble—no, four it cannot endure:
²² a slave who becomes a king,
   an overbearing fool who prospers,
²³ a bitter woman who finally gets a husband,
   a servant girl who supplants her mistress.

²⁴There are four things on earth that are small but unusually wise:
²⁵ Ants—they aren't strong,
   but they store up food for the winter.
²⁶ Rock badgers—they aren't powerful,
   but they make their homes among the rocky cliffs.
²⁷ Locusts—they have no king,
   but they march like an army in ranks.
²⁸ Lizards—they are easy to catch,
   but they are found even in kings' palaces.

²⁹There are three stately monarchs on the earth—no, four:
³⁰ the lion, king of animals, who won't turn aside for
   anything,
³¹ the strutting rooster,
   the male goat,
   a king as he leads his army.

³²If you have been a fool by being proud or plotting evil, don't brag about it—cover your mouth with your hand in shame.
³³As the beating of cream yields butter, and a blow to the nose causes bleeding, so anger causes quarrels.

PSALM 145

A psalm of praise of David.

¹I will praise you, my God and King,
  and bless your name forever and ever.
²I will bless you every day,
  and I will praise you forever.
³Great is the LORD! He is most worthy of praise!
  His greatness is beyond discovery!

⁴Let each generation tell its children
  of your mighty acts.
⁵I will meditate on your majestic, glorious splendor
  and your wonderful miracles.
⁶Your awe-inspiring deeds will be on every tongue;
  I will proclaim your greatness.
⁷Everyone will share the story of your wonderful
      goodness;
  they will sing with joy of your righteousness.

⁸The LORD is kind and merciful,

slow to get angry, full of unfailing love.

⁹The LORD is good to everyone.

He showers compassion on all his creation.

¹⁰All of your works will thank you, LORD,

and your faithful followers will bless you.

¹¹They will talk together about the glory of your kingdom;

they will celebrate examples of your power.

¹²They will tell about your mighty deeds

and about the majesty and glory of your reign.

¹³For your kingdom is an everlasting kingdom.

You rule generation after generation.

The LORD is faithful in all he says;

he is gracious in all he does.

¹⁴The LORD helps the fallen

and lifts up those bent beneath their loads.

¹⁵All eyes look to you for help;

you give them their food as they need it.

¹⁶When you open your hand,

you satisfy the hunger and thirst of every living thing.

¹⁷The LORD is righteous in everything he does;

he is filled with kindness.

[18]The Lord is close to all who call on him,
　　yes, to all who call on him sincerely.
[19]He fulfills the desires of those who fear him;
　　he hears their cries for help and rescues them.
[20]The Lord protects all those who love him,
　　but he destroys the wicked.

[21]I will praise the Lord,
　　and everyone on earth will bless his holy name
　　forever and forever.

Psalm 146

[1]Praise the Lord!

Praise the Lord, I tell myself.
[2]I will praise the Lord as long as I live.
　　I will sing praises to my God even with my dying breath.

[3]Don't put your confidence in powerful people;
　　there is no help for you there.
[4]When their breathing stops, they return to the earth,
　　and in a moment all their plans come to an end.
[5]But happy are those who have the God of Israel as their
　　　　helper,
　　whose hope is in the Lord their God.

⁶He is the one who made heaven and earth,
the sea, and everything in them.
He is the one who keeps every promise forever,
⁷   who gives justice to the oppressed
and food to the hungry.
The LORD frees the prisoners.
⁸   The LORD opens the eyes of the blind.
The LORD lifts the burdens of those bent beneath their loads.
The LORD loves the righteous.
⁹The LORD protects the foreigners among us.
He cares for the orphans and widows,
but he frustrates the plans of the wicked.

¹⁰The LORD will reign forever.
O Jerusalem, your God is King in every generation!

Praise the LORD!

PSALM 147

¹Praise the LORD!

How good it is to sing praises to our God!
How delightful and how right!
²The LORD is rebuilding Jerusalem
and bringing the exiles back to Israel.

³He heals the brokenhearted,
     binding up their wounds.
⁴He counts the stars
     and calls them all by name.
⁵How great is our Lord! His power is absolute!
     His understanding is beyond comprehension!
⁶The LORD supports the humble,
     but he brings the wicked down into the dust.

⁷Sing out your thanks to the LORD;
     sing praises to our God, accompanied by harps.
⁸He covers the heavens with clouds,
     provides rain for the earth,
     and makes the green grass grow in mountain pastures.
⁹He feeds the wild animals,
     and the young ravens cry to him for food.
¹⁰The strength of a horse does not impress him;
     how puny in his sight is the strength of a man.
¹¹Rather, the LORD's delight is in those who honor him,
     those who put their hope in his unfailing love.

¹²Praise the LORD, O Jerusalem!
     Praise your God, O Zion!
¹³For he has fortified the bars of your gates
     and blessed your children within you.

¹⁴He sends peace across your nation
and satisfies you with plenty of the finest wheat.
¹⁵He sends his orders to the world—
how swiftly his word flies!
¹⁶He sends the snow like white wool;
he scatters frost upon the ground like ashes.
¹⁷He hurls the hail like stones.
Who can stand against his freezing cold?
¹⁸Then, at his command, it all melts.
He sends his winds, and the ice thaws.

¹⁹He has revealed his words to Jacob,
his principles and laws to Israel.
²⁰He has not done this with any other nation;
they do not know his laws.

Praise the LORD!

PSALM 148

¹Praise the LORD!

Praise the LORD from the heavens!
Praise him from the skies!
²Praise him, all his angels!
Praise him, all the armies of heaven!

³Praise him, sun and moon!

    Praise him, all you twinkling stars!

⁴Praise him, skies above!

    Praise him, vapors high above the clouds!

⁵Let every created thing give praise to the LORD,

    for he issued his command, and they came into being.

⁶He established them forever and forever.

    His orders will never be revoked.

⁷Praise the LORD from the earth,

    you creatures of the ocean depths,

⁸fire and hail, snow and storm,

    wind and weather that obey him,

⁹mountains and all hills,

    fruit trees and all cedars,

¹⁰wild animals and all livestock,

    reptiles and birds,

¹¹kings of the earth and all people,

    rulers and judges of the earth,

¹²young men and maidens,

    old men and children.

¹³Let them all praise the name of the LORD.

    For his name is very great;

    his glory towers over the earth and heaven!

¹⁴He has made his people strong,

honoring his godly ones—
the people of Israel who are close to him.

Praise the LORD!

PSALM 149

¹Praise the LORD!

Sing to the LORD a new song.
 Sing his praises in the assembly of the faithful.
²O Israel, rejoice in your Maker.
 O people of Jerusalem, exult in your King.
³Praise his name with dancing,
 accompanied by tambourine and harp.
⁴For the LORD delights in his people;
 he crowns the humble with salvation.
⁵Let the faithful rejoice in this honor.
 Let them sing for joy as they lie on their beds.
⁶Let the praises of God be in their mouths,
 and a sharp sword in their hands—
⁷to execute vengeance on the nations
 and punishment on the peoples,
⁸to bind their kings with shackles
 and their leaders with iron chains,
⁹to execute the judgment written against them.

This is the glory of his faithful ones.

Praise the LORD!

PSALM 150

¹Praise the LORD!

Praise God in his heavenly dwelling;
   praise him in his mighty heaven!
²Praise him for his mighty works;
   praise his unequaled greatness!
³Praise him with a blast of the trumpet;
   praise him with the lyre and harp!
⁴Praise him with the tambourine and dancing;
   praise him with stringed instruments and flutes!
⁵Praise him with a clash of cymbals;
   praise him with loud clanging cymbals.
⁶Let everything that lives sing praises to the LORD!

Praise the LORD!

PROVERBS 31

These are the sayings of King Lemuel, an oracle that his
mother taught him.

²O my son, O son of my womb, O son of my promises, ³do not spend your strength on women, on those who ruin kings.

⁴And it is not for kings, O Lemuel, to guzzle wine. Rulers should not crave liquor. ⁵For if they drink, they may forget their duties and be unable to give justice to those who are oppressed. ⁶Liquor is for the dying, and wine for those in deep depression. ⁷Let them drink to forget their poverty and remember their troubles no more.

⁸Speak up for those who cannot speak for themselves; ensure justice for those who are perishing. ⁹Yes, speak up for the poor and helpless, and see that they get justice.

¹⁰Who can find a virtuous and capable wife? She is worth more than precious rubies. ¹¹Her husband can trust her, and she will greatly enrich his life. ¹²She will not hinder him but help him all her life.

¹³She finds wool and flax and busily spins it. ¹⁴She is like a merchant's ship; she brings her food from afar. ¹⁵She gets up before dawn to prepare breakfast for her household and plan the day's work for her servant girls. ¹⁶She goes out to inspect a field and buys it; with her earnings she plants a vineyard.

¹⁷She is energetic and strong, a hard worker. ¹⁸She watches for bargains; her lights burn late into the night.

[19]Her hands are busy spinning thread, her fingers twisting fiber.

[20]She extends a helping hand to the poor and opens her arms to the needy.

[21]She has no fear of winter for her household because all of them have warm clothes. [22]She quilts her own bedspreads. She dresses like royalty in gowns of finest cloth.

[23]Her husband is well known, for he sits in the council meeting with the other civic leaders.

[24]She makes belted linen garments and sashes to sell to the merchants.

[25]She is clothed with strength and dignity, and she laughs with no fear of the future. [26]When she speaks, her words are wise, and kindness is the rule when she gives instructions. [27]She carefully watches all that goes on in her household and does not have to bear the consequences of laziness.

[28]Her children stand and bless her. Her husband praises her: [29]"There are many virtuous and capable women in the world, but you surpass them all!"

[30]Charm is deceptive, and beauty does not last; but a woman who fears the LORD will be greatly praised. [31]Reward her for all she has done. Let her deeds publicly declare her praise.